JOHN F. KENNEDY JR.

A Life in the Spotlight

JOHN F. KENNEDY JR.

A Life in the Spotlight

MICHAEL DRUITT

Ariel Books

Andrews McMeel Publishing
Kansas City

Library of Congress Cataloging-in-Publication Data

Druitt, Michael.
    John F. Kennedy Jr.: a life in the spotlight /
Michael Druitt
        p.   cm.
        Includes bibliographical references.
        ISBN 0-8362-1513-3 (ppb)
        1. Kennedy, John F. (John Fitzgerald), 1960–1999
        2. Children of presidents—United States—Biography.   I. Title.
E843.K42D78   1996
973.922' 092—dc20
[B]
                                                                                        96– 6271
                                                                                              CIP

Publisher wishes to express gratitude and appreciation to the following for photographic materials and research: The John Fitzgerald Kennedy Library and Donna Cotterell; Dorothy Whiting; Archive Photos; Fotos International/Archive Photos; Tom Gates/Archive Photos; Jerry Ohlinger's Movie Material Store, Inc.; Photofest; Star File and their photographers: Danny Chin, Dominick Conde, Brett Lee, Gene Shaw, Irv Steinberg, and Vinnie Zuffante; UPI/Corbis-Bettmann; Visualizations; Anthony Del-Prete; and Susan Ehrlich.

The text of this book is set in Garamond with Trajan and Bodega Serif display by Mspace, Katonah, New York.

C O N T E N T S

FOREWORD

EDITOR'S NOTE: When this book first went to press in 1996, John F. Kennedy Jr. and Carolyn Bessette had just married. As this book was going to press a second time, the plane that was carrying John, Carolyn, and her sister to Martha's Vineyard, Massachusetts, plunged into the sea. The author and publisher respectfully dedicate this book to the memory and spirit of these three young lives. This revised edition includes the following new foreword; the rest of the text is unchanged from the first edition.

On the night of July 16, 1999, John F. Kennedy Jr.'s private plane plummeted into the Atlantic Ocean, taking his life along with the lives of his beautiful wife, Carolyn Bessette Kennedy, and her sister Lauren Bessette. What was once the optimistic tale of dynamic young lives filled with unlimited promise became, instead, another tragic chapter in the seemingly endless saga of Kennedy sorrows. Countless dreams crashed along with John's plane, and the nation mourned the loss.

On their way to attend the Hyannis Port wedding of John's cousin Rory Kennedy, John and Carolyn had intended to land on Martha's Vineyard just long enough to drop Lauren off. But before their plane reached the Vineyard, it dived sharply into the dark ocean and vanished from radar screens. Family members who had gathered in Hyannis Port to celebrate Rory's wedding (which was postponed indefinitely) turned, instead, to grieve another terrible loss.

John and the slender, elegant Carolyn were among the most glamorous of their generation. Still, they chose to live simply in their New York City loft, getting to know their neighbors and frequenting the local bar and coffee shop. Within hours of the tragic news, candles, bouquets of flowers, and handwritten notes began to appear on the steps outside their apartment building.

In the years after his marriage to Carolyn, John had followed his own path, working hard to develop his iconoclastic political magazine, *George,* while avoiding all political overtures including, reportedly, an invitation to run for the U.S. Senate seat in New York vacated by Senator Daniel Patrick Moynihan.

In John F. Kennedy Jr., the world will remember a handsome, generous young man who was determined to live a meaningful life on his own terms, in spite of the clamoring demands of celebrity and a birthright of power that might have unleashed arrogance in a lesser man. His death left his sister, Caroline Kennedy Schlossberg, the only survivor of the family dream that Jacqueline Kennedy Onassis once dubbed Camelot.

As the Kennedy and Bessette families struggled to come to terms with their losses, Senator Edward Kennedy told the world, "[John] was a devoted husband to Carolyn, a loving brother to Caroline, an amazing uncle to her children, a close and dear friend to his cousins, and a beloved nephew to my sisters and me. He was the adored son of two proud parents whom he now joins with God. We loved him deeply, and his loss leaves an enormous void in all our lives."

PREFATORY NOTE

The public has long labored under the delusion that John Fitzgerald Kennedy Jr. was called John-John by the family. John Jr. was never called John-John by anyone but the press. A reporter once misheard the president calling his son, and he assumed, and reported, that JFK had said "John-John." He had not, but the name stuck, and even now people use the misnomer. He himself usually goes by John Kennedy. Throughout this book he shall be John, John Jr., or John Fitzgerald Kennedy Jr., depending on the context, and his father will be Jack, JFK, the president, or John Fitzgerald Kennedy.

STILL STANDING

JOHN FITZGERALD KENNEDY Jr. was born on November 25, 1960, two and a half weeks after his father was elected president of the United States, less than two months before his father was inaugurated. Three years later, that father, murdered by an assassin's bullet, was buried on John's third birthday. Twenty years after that, he graduated from Brown University on the fifteenth anniversary of the assassination of his uncle Robert F. Kennedy.

Assassination, and the threat of assassination, has haunted the Kennedy family for an entire generation now, and it has shadowed John throughout his life, although he refuses to let it worry him.[1] There have been death threats against him; against his mother; against his older sister, Caroline; and against various members of the larger family, especially his uncle Ted. Until he was sixteen years old, he was guarded by members of the Secret Service every day of his life. They were often necessary merely to bat away the spectators and reporters and photographers who considered it their right and duty to pester him.

When he graduated from Phillips Exeter Academy in Andover, Massachusetts, legions of photographers virtually trampled people to get to him. As a friend of his said of that occasion, "After experiencing about twenty minutes of what it meant to be John, I really sympathized with his having to cope with all that attention every day of his life."[2] That, however, was par for the course, one of the inescapable corollaries of being John F. Kennedy Jr. Yet to most people, who he is, is far less important than what he represents.

John F. Kennedy, for at least the last three years of his life (and the first three years of his

(above) John in New York City

(opposite) John swimming, July 1986

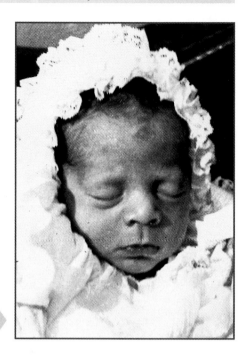

*John at two weeks,
December 1960*

> "Millions of
>
> American
>
> mothers . . .
>
> monitor[ed]
>
> the progress
>
> of baby
>
> Kennedy
>
> as if he were
>
> their own."

son's), was the most famous man in the world and remains so perhaps even now, over thirty years after his death. Jacqueline Bouvier Kennedy, for those three years and many more to follow, was unquestionably the world's most famous (and admired) woman. His sister Caroline was the most famous girl and he was the most famous boy.

Throughout much of his life John Jr. could not walk out the door of his house, apartment, or dormitory without running the risk of being accosted, photographed, or asked to sign autographs—even at three in the morning. Today if he takes his shirt off in Central Park (which he often does), the world not only knows it but sees it. If he travels to almost any city of the world, flunks an exam, or dines in a fashionable restaurant (or even a Chinatown hole-in-the-wall), that fact is recorded in dozens, perhaps hundreds, conceivably thousands of newspapers and magazines and TV tabloid and news shows across the globe. He can have no secrets; his life, simply because of who (or rather what) he is, is virtually devoid of privacy.

On the event of John's first birthday, American citizens were miffed because they were not allowed to take their own pictures of him and had to make do with prints of the official photographs. "Millions of American mothers . . . monitor[ed] the progress of baby Kennedy as if he were their own."[3] And when "baby Kennedy" was only a little older and his mother allowed his hair to grow long in Little Lord Fauntleroy fashion, irate citizens flooded the White House with cards and letters, some filled with money; they wanted John to have a "proper" haircut.

At five, he went skinny-dipping on vacation; that act made headlines. When he went trick-or-treating with friends at Halloween, plainclothes Secret Service agents trailed behind him. As a boy in New York, he had to run a gauntlet of reporters in order to

John leads Caroline through a crowd of media and onlookers after Jackie's death, May 1994

make it to school, and even in school he and his acquaintances were pestered relentlessly by news squirrels and ordinary citizens who wanted to know all about him and his family. As a teenager he was so mobbed at a screening of *Saturday Night Fever* that even John Travolta, the film's idolized star, was left wondering where his adoring audience had gone.

It sounds like a life scripted by Robert Ludlum or by Ian Fleming (his father's favorite author) in a particularly grim but gleeful mood. But of course it has its compensations: He is a millionaire. He is a Kennedy. He receives adulation worldwide, but above all in his own country, which some people believe his family should rule as a birthright. Women throw themselves at him daily, as do sharks, hustlers, and Hollywood pitchmen who want him to play his father in films, along with legitimate movers and shakers in politics, law, finance, society, the arts, and almost every other field.

His family name is legend, one of the most powerful and influential in the history of this country, and to this day many people look to him to redeem America from its current doldrums. His cousins are the sons and daughters of past or present senators, but he is the son of a former president. Some of those cousins have been involved in drug and sex scandals, but he has remained unscathed. He is the Shining Prince, Prince Charming, and the heir apparent. Many considered him the heir eventual from the moment he was born.

He does not have to work, although he does. If he wrote a novel it would be the subject of a major publishing bidding war, however wretched it might be. (And if it were brilliant, we would take for granted that someone had written it for him.) If he started a law firm, the gliterati of whatever city it happened to be based in (and perhaps many others as well) would fight to become his clients. He can do anything he wants or nothing at all—and even if he does nothing, the world will still kill to throw him presents.

On top of all this John is personable, charming, unpretentious, athletic, and impossibly handsome, with the "matinée idol" looks of his father, but he's darker, more intense, and therefore even

> "After experiencing about twenty minutes of what it meant to be John, I really sympathized with his having to cope with all that attention every day of his life."

John, December 1963

John and Jackie arrive home in New York City after skiing in Colorado, March 1968

more swashbuckling. He had every reason in the world to become an unbearable snob but did not: not even his enemies (who are enemies mostly through jealousy) have accused him of that. Nor is he spoiled, bratty, or driven to self-destruction. He seems impossible, in short, and yet he exists.

But still the question must be asked, Would you want to trade places with this man? Could you bear to be in the spotlight *every day of your life?* Could you deal with the fact that every meal you

John's first day on the job as a prosecutor at the Manhattan district attorney's office, November 1990

John Kennedy is not only very rich: He is the last great knight of Camelot . . .

eat in a public place and every book you buy or magazine you subscribe to, will likely be recorded somewhere? That the title of any video you rent might appear in the *National Enquirer?* He is photographed at ATMs getting money; it is front-page news when he acts up in public. How many people could live such a life—and he is now thirty-five years old—without losing their grip on reality?

And yet John Kennedy has come through all this with extraordinary grace, patience, charm, style, and even wit. When a lawyer said on national television that the rape trial of William Kennedy Smith, one of John's closest friends in all of his enormous extended family, symbolized "the fall of the house of Kennedy," John sent the lawyer chrysanthemums and a note: "Still standing, baby. Best, The House of Kennedy."

F. Scott Fitzgerald once wrote that the very rich are different from you and me. John Kennedy is not only very rich: He is the last great knight of Camelot, the man who so many hope will be able to restore the fabled kingdom his father and mother established. In so hoping, of course, they deny him his humanity and individuality and turn him into a symbol: the Redeemer, the Shining Prince, the Next Kennedy.

Who is John Kennedy? Does he want to be president? If not, just what does he want to do? He is still in the process of defining himself and discovering the answers to those questions, but since his life thus far has been one of the most public in history, we know a good deal that might hint at the possibilities. To tell his story, however, and to understand the pressures that bind him, we must begin with his family.

John and actress Daryl Hannah are mobbed by reporters at the Manila airport on their way to Hong Kong, August 1993

THE KENNEDY DYNASTY

KENNEDYS AND FITZGERALDS: THE FOREBEARS

The Kennedy dynasty began in nineteenth-century Boston with two families whose forebears had recently emigrated from Ireland: those of Patrick Joseph Kennedy, known throughout his life as P. J., and John Fitzgerald, known as Honey Fitz.

P. J. was a saloon keeper who worked hard, prospered, and was a trusted friend to the immigrant Irish community, whose members were for the most part poor and exploited by the Brahmins who dominated the city. P. J. gave them advice, lent them money, helped them to find jobs and housing, and eventually entered politics as a member of the Democratic machine. He never forgot his roots or abandoned his principles (or his people, to whom he was an idol); although he became one of the most powerful figures in Massachusetts politics, he never tried to appease the Brahmins, who despised any and all Irish merely because they were Irish. The same could not be said for the most ambitious and successful of his sons, Joseph, born in 1888.

Honey Fitz was a more traditional politician who aspired to the respect and privileges of the city's Protestant elite. Unlike P. J., he was interested more in power than in people, and those he served were generally those who might serve him in return. In 1906 he made history by becoming the first Irishman elected mayor of Boston. Honey Fitz was savagely dedicated to winning, winning anything and everything, at all costs, and he passed this obsessive drive on to his daughter, Rose, born in 1890. It was one of several traits that linked her to Joseph Kennedy, whom she married in October 1914. They in turn instilled this ideal into their nine children,

(above) P. J. Kennedy, late 1880s
(opposite) John "Honey Fitz" Fitzgerald

all of whom were programmed to triumph in everything they attempted, no matter how trivial. Three of them rank among the most famous politicians of our time: John Fitzgerald, Robert Fitzgerald, and Edward Moore (Ted).

JOSEPH KENNEDY: THE ARCHITECT

Joe Kennedy lacked his father's compassion, his feeling for people, and his loyalty above all to his fellow Irish. P. J. had built his reputation by listening to people's troubles while tending bar and helping them in whatever way he could; Joe built his by exploiting any situation or person to amass greater power and wealth.

He felt no particular ties to his Irish community. Indeed, Joe seemed to resent his heritage to some extent because in the Boston of his childhood the Irish were still the lowest of the low. Jobs were offered with the proviso, "Mad dogs and Irishmen need not apply"; and the Brahmins who ruled the city could sometimes not even be bothered to waste contempt on the city's Irish citizens.

Joe was, if anything, even more single-minded and driven than his future father-in-law, Honey Fitz. Joe, too, felt that winning was the final measure of a man and wealth was the best proof that one had conquered, so he set himself with grim efficiency to two principal tasks: taking the modest wealth accumulated by his father and turning it into a vast fortune (in this he succeeded brilliantly) and forcing the Brahmins of Boston (and, by extension, of the world) to accept and respect him. The results were mixed. To those whose ancestors arrived on the *Mayflower* or even to those who accumulated their fortunes in the eighteenth century, the Kennedys were nouveaux riches. Garry Wills makes a very acute point about Joe, his womanizing, and the strata of society he chose to invade:

> After his rejection by the Brahmins of Boston, he oriented his world around New York and Hollywood, around the sports and journalism and cinema stars of the roaring twenties. A starlet would have disgraced the better Boston families; but Kennedy displayed his actresses as so many decorations, as signs that he was looking to new centers of power and of popular acclaim. The Boston gentry were exclusive. He would be expansive, open and racy. He was steering his family down the course that made them staples of the tabloids.[4]

"He was steering his family down the course that made them staples of the tabloids."

Joseph Kennedy Sr. (right) en route to Europe with two friends, 1912

As a youth Joe worked various odd jobs, from stove lighter to delivery boy for a fashionable hatter; after graduation from Harvard (which was only beginning to admit Catholics and Jews and still would not allow his kind into its better clubs) he worked for a newspaper and ran sightseeing tours, then took a job with a bank. There he learned the intricacies of business and high finance. Later he ventured into real estate, where he specialized in buying up mortgages, evicting the low-income families who held them, and refurbishing the houses and reselling them at a considerable profit. His was a very different attitude from his father's.

But, undeniably, it worked. Joe eventually bought a part interest in a trust company, which not only helped to make him wealthy but also secured him a wife. He had known Rose

Fitzgerald for years, but her father had always been skeptical and even contemptuous of the Kennedys: They were merely politicians, after all, whereas he was the mayor of Boston. The origins of both families had been similar in their lowliness; however, while P. J. Kennedy was more honest and admirable than Honey Fitz, the Fitzgeralds had risen higher and now Honey Fitz ran the city. Once Joe elevated himself as a respectable banker, though, he became worthy of the hand of the mayor's treasured eldest daughter and the two were married on October 7, 1914.

The First World War strikingly revealed the mercenary in Joe's character, because he was against it—not for noble pacific reasons but because war interfered with the business of making money. Once the United States entered the conflict in 1917, many of Joe's contemporaries, who were busy joining the armed services, scorned him. He could not have cared less. Joe had his own purpose and his own vision of the future, so he became general manager at a shipyard. There he did a wizardly job of producing destroyers for the war effort, although he also used his political connections to dodge the draft. In this, as in all his endeavors, he made money and ran roughshod over people in order to do it.

Joe Kennedy was disciplined, intelligent, and highly creative. He also, as was his wont, pushed ethics to the limit: After the war he worked for an investment banking firm and mastered the stock market, where he "used inside information . . . to make himself a millionaire."[5]

He never specialized in any field, unlike most of the earlier American robber barons, who created gigantic fortunes in steel or railroads or banking and stuck sedulously to their one area of expertise until their fabulous wealth was secure. Joe flirted with a business, made a quick profit or even a killing, and then plowed his money into another field, where he made even more money, and so on, until even he had made enough to be satisfied. Yet Joe could never truly be satisfied with anything. Notes Garry Wills:

> He had no credentials but his latest achievement—no community to lean back on, no base but the one he forged for himself every day, the clearing he made for his family in a hostile environment. The endless catechizing of his children on the need to win, the competitive edge he sharpened in each of them, reflected his own inner urgencies. If he did not keep winning, there was nothing to support him. The dragonfly, with nothing to light on, would just fall straight down forever.[6]

Joe Sr. and Rose in Palm Beach, Florida, 1923

Joe Sr. and Rose on their wedding day, October 1914

(top) Joe Sr. and Rose return home from Europe

(bottom) Joe Sr. and movie magnate Jesse Lasky, 1924

Background photo: Gloria Swanson

His was a classic American rise to power, and later in the decade this dragonfly invaded the ultimate pit of glamour: Hollywood. Joe's rich portfolio included a string of theaters, and he quickly recognized that immense profits could be made in the "dream business," which already was extraordinarily popular across the globe. Joe also realized that as much clout could be wielded through the distribution of pictures (after they were made, they had to be shown) as through their production, so he rapidly purchased a distribution company (in typical fashion: for a fraction of its worth), cut corners, made mincemeat of ethics, gouged his partners, lived in fabulous luxury, and eventually became a film producer and financier. And he began an affair with Gloria Swanson, one of the film capital's greatest stars at the time; their affair was facilitated by the fact that he now lived in California while his family remained in Boston—though that, in fact, would have made no real difference in the end.

This affair initiated another tradition that Joe passed on to several of his children and grandchildren. Jack Kennedy had numerous affairs with Hollywood actresses (such as Angie Dickinson and Marilyn Monroe, who also had an affair with Robert Kennedy); so, more recently, has John Jr. (Sarah Jessica Parker and Darryl Hannah). One of Joe's younger daughters, Patricia, married film star Peter Lawford and Hollywood glitz has threaded throughout the Kennedy saga ever since Joe's very open affair with the diva. JFK in particular adored the movies; he even telephoned the set when *Advise and Consent* was under production to see if he could get an early print.

Joe always seemed to know when to cut and run, which led to one of his greatest coups. After the Wall Street crash on October 29, 1929, when other investors were terrified and confused, Joe bought up stock at a tiny fraction of its value, and by 1930, with the Great Depression under way, he was worth over $100 million. Joe, as always, was very shrewd: He realized that big business, which until then had been the most potent force in American society, was now in disarray, and that the power was shifting to Washington. He shifted with it.

Through his generous financial contributions to the Democratic Party, Joe helped elect Franklin Delano Roosevelt to the presidency. In return, he was named treasurer of the United States, but this title brought more honor than influence and Joe

Joe Sr.

was furious. Eventually he was put in charge of the Securities and Exchange Commission (SEC), where he did an excellent job of closing the kind of loopholes that had helped him to become so phenomenally rich. In 1937 he was appointed chairman of the Maritime Commission, where his work was as diligent and thorough as it had been at the shipyard and the SEC.

Still he wanted more. Indeed, he wanted to become president, but Roosevelt was shrewd enough to preempt Joe's more threatening moves without ever alienating him enough to cause an open rift. Late in 1937 he gave Kennedy the job of his dreams: ambassador to the Court of St. James's. The Boston Irishman was soon presented to the king and queen of England. It proved to be Joe's ultimate triumph and his most bitter defeat. (It also kept him out of the country, where he might have challenged Roosevelt's renomination, and out of the public eye, which was perhaps more important to Roosevelt than anything else.)

Ambassadors are supposed to communicate and carry out the wishes of their president; instead, Joe Kennedy fought Roosevelt at every turn. Kennedy was antiwar, albeit for purely venal reasons, but Roosevelt was maneuvering to aid England in its struggle in the war he knew was inevitable and quietly positioning his own

Joe always seemed to know when to cut and run . . .

(top) Kathleen, Rose, and Rosemary appear before the Court of St. James's, 1938

Rose, Joe Sr., and the children (except for Joe Jr. who is at college) in Rome for the coronation of Pope Pius XII, 1939

(left) Jack, Joe Sr., and Joe Jr. en route to England, 1938

(above) The family in Palm Beach, Christmas 1937

country to enter it at some date as yet unknown. His ambassador, however, worked to serve only his own purposes, not those of his boss, and the president was livid. Kennedy was indignant and felt increasingly isolated; in October 1940 he demanded to be recalled.

A month later, with Roosevelt's triumphant reelection to an unprecedented third term, Joe Kennedy's own presidential ambitions, which had been simmering for years, were effectively laid to rest. His ruthless will and desire continued unabated, however, and now he focused it on his sons. The eldest, Joe Jr., was accordingly groomed for power, but on August 12, 1944, he was killed in a mysterious plane accident over France. Attention then concentrated on the second son: John Fitzgerald Kennedy.

ROSE: THE MATRIARCH

Young Rose Kennedy was the unofficial First Lady of Boston while her father was mayor, because she delighted in hoopla and attention, which her retiring mother did not. Rose was personable, athletic, highly independent, and as ruthless and dedicated to winning as her father.

She was also, however, a girl, and as such was subjected to very strict discipline not only by her mother at home but also by a variety of nuns in a succession of convent schools. Rose "rebelled" by becoming excessively pious on the outside, for which she is well

known, but cold and aloof on the inside. For all the publicity we have seen about the Kennedy clannishness and happiness over the years, the children of Joe and Rose were given remarkably little affection throughout their lives. The one "value" drummed incessantly into their heads was to win, win constantly, at all costs. "We don't want any losers around here," Joe was famous for saying. "In this family we want winners."[7] This "philosophy" reverberates through a far-flung and, in many respects, broken family even now ("hardly a recipe for relaxed and self-confident children," as Nigel Hamilton dryly notes), and it was given its ultimate expression when Joe quietly had Rosemary, his eldest daughter, lobotomized. Rosemary was mildly retarded, but Joe felt she was hopeless. After the lobotomy, she was. (Rose was out of town when it happened, but it is an open question whether she would have done anything against the move or not. Certainly she betrayed no outrage or horror when she finally learned.)[8] After this tragedy, Rosemary was sent to a Catholic nursing home—not in Massachusetts or even New England or New York (where the Kennedys had houses) but in Wisconsin, where they had no connections at all.

Rose en route to Europe, 1911

Honey Fitz and Rose en route to South America

Rose, like her husband-to-be, was bitterly snubbed by Boston society and came to despise it. Her official society debut was a glittering event attended by governors and congressmen and even declared a city holiday by her father, but the Brahmins still ignored her and refused to invite her to join their almost entirely Protestant clubs. Rose retaliated by forming her own—which was even more exclusive than theirs.

To some extent she was also ignored by her husband, who was always busy making money, usually behind closed doors, and who rarely socialized, as her father had done. Rose once had presided over glamorous dinners and balls but now her sole duty was to look after her children. (There would be nine in all: Joe Jr., Jack, Rosemary, Kathleen, Eunice, Patricia, Robert, Jean, and Edward.) At times she seems to have resented them. Certainly her marriage was unhappy.

So Rose withdrew. She withdrew sometimes literally, spending hours a day in her own private rooms or bungalows, but she with-

> "In this family we want winners."

Rosemary and Jack in Cohasset, Massachusetts, circa 1923

(above) Rose with Joe Jr., Rosemary, and Jack

(right) Rose

"John Jr. consistently viewed his grandmother through a prism of happy memories."

drew emotionally as well. She played at being the perfect wife and mother, raising her children strictly and with close attention to their desperate need to succeed, but most of it was an act. Even when Joe traveled east from Hollywood and openly conducted his affair with Gloria Swanson, Rose maintained a placid demeanor and pretended that she and the actress were the best of friends. Her children saw how her wildly unfaithful husband cheated on her and how she reacted. What conclusions they drew from this can only be guessed at—but her sons were philanderers, and most of her daughters married such.

Yet among certain of her grandchildren, at least, Rose was very popular. She gave them constant advice on their behavior and education and on religious matters, and her efforts seem to have been appreciated. Caroline named her first daughter Rose, and

in later years, John Jr. consistently viewed his grandmother through a prism of happy memories. Rose encouraged her grandchildren to put pen to paper, and when he was twelve, John composed a testament to his grandmother, writing of how much she had taught him, of how bad his father had been as a little boy, how much they laughed together—and how much he enjoyed her Boston cream pie.[9]

Rose with Eunice, Kathleen, Rosemary, Jack, and Joe Jr., 1921

The family in Hyannis Port, 1931

THE KENNEDY TRAGEDY

ON AUGUST 12, 1944, Joseph Kennedy Jr., who was flying sorties against the launching of the German V-1 rockets devastating Britain, took his plane up, switched to remote control, and was immediately blown to pieces. Mystery has surrounded his death ever since.

There was no need for him to fly that day. He had volunteered, but so had several other pilots. When they were informed, however, that the electrical circuits were dangerous and a single day more would allow the electronics engineer to rectify the problem, every one of them, with the exception of Joe Jr., decided to wait. Some of his fellow pilots believed he had a death wish;[10] others familiar with the family suggest that he may have been impelled "to disprove the charge, common among the British, that the Kennedys were 'yellow.' (During the Nazi blitz the ambassador [Joseph Kennedy] had spent evenings outside London to escape danger.)"[11] Barbara Gibson (who spent ten years as Rose's secretary) has gone so far as to argue that it may have been a deliberate suicide attempt;[12] yet virtually all commentators agree that Joe Jr. was depressed over the sudden fame and success of the dashing Jack, who had recently been awarded a medal and an oceanful of publicity for saving the lives of three of his men (the famous *PT-109* incident), and that Joe Jr. was desperate to compete against and *beat* his little brother. According to this theory, Joe Jr. believed he, as the eldest, should have been the first and best to glory, so he was despondent when he "failed."

Kathleen, the next-oldest daughter, nick-

(above) Joe Jr. in England, 1942

(opposite) Pat, Eunice, Jean, Bobby, and Joe Jr. playing in the snow in Bronxville, New York, 1936

named Kick, rebelled in her own way. To the horror of her piously Catholic mother, she married the marquis of Huntington, an English Protestant; and when he was killed in the war, she had an affair with, and eventually planned to marry, another English Protestant. Instead, in 1948, she herself died in a plane crash with her fiancé while they were on their way to seek her father's blessing; and because Rose believed that her daughter was in purgatory and deserved the punishment she had received, she refused to attend the funeral. Jack was one of the very few who seemed to be shocked by these events—and he himself paid another price.

Jack was the only one of the Kennedy children without a

Joe Jr., 1936

Kathleen and the Marquis of Huntington, on their wedding day, 1944

*Kathleen with Winston
and Clementine Churchill
in Palm Beach, 1946*

robust and sturdy frame to accompany his vaulting need to win. That, nevertheless, did not stop him: In their endless football games and other frolics, he slammed as mercilessly against his brothers and sisters as they did against him, even when he could barely walk because of chronic back pain.

Undoubtedly there was an element of heroism in Joe Jr.'s death, as there was in the physical agony Jack suffered throughout his life, of which voters knew next to nothing. But what kind of family produces children so competitive that they feel humiliated, and perhaps even brood over death, when a younger sibling is more successful? What kind of family insists that even a quasi-invalid brother must compete with berserk frenzy on the playing field? Ted Kennedy, who may have been the most gifted of all the children (we can never know, since his brothers all died so young) and who has arguably achieved the most, has been in a hopeless and self-defeating competition throughout his life against slain idols Bobby and Jack. As Garry Wills notes:

> [Ted] has to keep living three lives at once—or keep giving an account of the lives the other men lived for him. Walking through his empty house, crammed with pictures of the family, one realizes how much of his life has already been lived for him, off in directions he can neither take, anymore, nor renounce.[13]

Jack, Jean, Rose, Joe Sr., Pat, Bobby, Eunice, and Teddy (holding football) in Hyannis Port, 1948

Jack, Rose, and Honey Fitz,
July 1946

This was exactly the sort of shackling Wills had in mind when he so eloquently called his book *The Kennedy Imprisonment*—and yet was it *impossible* for a man of Ted Kennedy's intelligence to escape? Was it inevitable that he capitulate to the family demons? Perhaps. Those demons appear to have exerted immense power.

The Kennedys, including Ted, have been haunted by tragedy throughout the "second generation" (the children of Joe and Rose), and a certain morbidity strongly colors the third. Alcoholism, drug abuse, sexual excess, and scandals of every sort thread throughout the lives of "the Kennedy cousins," but two who seem largely free of the taint are Caroline and John Jr. They, too, have had their ups and downs, but on the whole, and especially in comparison with so many (though by no means all) of their cousins, they appear remarkably level-headed and free of scandal. One can only speculate that much of this stems from the fact that JFK, whatever lovelessness may have wracked him throughout his childhood, was an adoring father—and that their mother strove relentlessly to make sure they were as removed as possible from the influence of the Kennedy clan.

Jacqueline Kennedy was a Bouvier and wanted her children to be the same. When she married into the family, however, not even she realized quite what she was in for. One did not marry a Kennedy: One married the entire family. Jackie did her best to change that, but swimming against the Kennedy tide, as many have discovered to their peril, was currying almost certain defeat.

> One did not marry a Kennedy: One married the entire family.

JACK AND JACKIE

KENNEDY

John Fitzgerald Kennedy never wanted to be president; he had always dreamed of being a writer (and purportedly wanted to run a newspaper when his political career was over). What he wanted did not matter, however: He and his siblings were there to do their father's bidding ("Jack Kennedy shook hands with his father by making a power salute; the younger Kennedy would make a fist, and the elder Kennedy would wrap his hand around it"[14]). Joe was determined that one of his sons would become leader of the country. Jack dutifully did as he was told, and both of them were fortunate: JFK was the perfect candidate.

He was photogenic, lithe (despite his crippling back troubles, which almost killed him on at least one occasion), and brimming with charm; he was quick, vigorous, and as handsome as Tyrone Power. Jack was one of those people who brought a new and special light into a room merely by entering it, and both men and women were dazzled by him—especially when he cracked his boyish grin.

But there was more: He was also a writer and a man of current affairs. In 1940, fresh out of Harvard, he had written an analysis of the current political situation called *Why England Slept*. In fact, the "book" was a threadbare expansion of his senior thesis, stuffed with statistics and inside information provided by his ambassador/father, rewritten by Arthur Krock, Joe's journalist friend, and with an introduction by none other than Henry Luce, the magnate behind the Time-Life empire. Despite all this muscle, the book had little impact. But it was on the résumé, and more—and better—was to come.

Yet far more germane and impressive both

(above) Jack in Hyannis Port, 1946

(opposite) Jack and Jackie (then his fiancée), June 1953

to Joe and to voters was the fact that Jack Kennedy was a war hero. His PT boat had been cut in two by a Japanese destroyer, and he had rescued three of his men at the risk of his own life. (He actually had rescued only one, which was certainly heroic enough, but the Kennedy publicity machine augmented the number, as it augmented almost everything. *Always* with the Kennedys there would be a disjunction between the depiction of the truth and the truth, even when the truth was perfectly honorable.) Jack's success in politics seemed ordained; indeed, John Fitzgerald Kennedy, who had been drilled in the ignominy of failure since childhood, never lost an election, except when he ran for the Democratic vice presidential nomination in 1956. (And even that turned out to be a victory in disguise, because the Democratic ticket was crushed by Eisenhower-Nixon that November and had Jack been a part of the debacle, his Catholicism would almost certainly have been blamed; then he might never have been heard from again.)

Jack and the rest of the PT-109 crew off Guadalcanal, circa 1943

He entered Congress in 1946, the same year as Richard Nixon—with whom he was a friendly rival for a while. After serving for three terms, he successfully ran for the Senate in 1952. Kennedy had everything: youth, looks, money, power, boundless reservoirs of self-confidence—and as many women as Medusa had snakes. He was becoming notorious for his bachelor revels and the endless string of women associated with his name. His father, from whom he had inherited his insatiable ways, was beginning to worry. Up to a point such randy activity was amusing; beyond that point it began to look bad. Jack was being groomed for the

Pat, Teddy, Rose, Bobby, Eunice, and Jack in Hyannis Port

presidency and everybody knew it, but a president must have a wife—and the women he was dating (actresses, models, divorcées, non-Catholics) were uniformly unsuitable.

Then he was introduced to Jacqueline Bouvier, and Joe's worries ended. Jackie came from wealth, although she possessed little money herself; she belonged to the upper crust of American

*Honey Fitz, Joe Sr.,
and Jack, 1946*

society. She was pretty, stylish, and well-bred and had attended all the finest schools. Best of all, she was Catholic. (Joe was convinced, rightly or wrongly, that his son could never be elected president if he did not marry a Catholic.) To add icing to the cake, she was *French* Catholic, which somehow seemed more appealing than Irish Catholic, especially to a man like Joe. It was a marriage made in heaven, or at least in Joe's back rooms, which was just as good, and Jack dutifully did as he was ordered.

Was it as cynical as that? It seems to have been. If Jack ever really loved any woman it was probably Inga Arvad, a Danish-born actress and newspaper correspondent with whom he conducted a torrid affair during the war; his father forcibly broke off the liaison because Inga—promiscuous, independent, oft-married, foreign, non-Catholic, almost too beautiful, and suspected (unfairly) by the FBI of being a Nazi spy—might well have been the worst possible female as far as Joe's vicarious presidential ambitions were concerned. Jack, when asked by a friend years later if he had ever fallen "desperately, hopelessly in love, . . . just shrugged and said, 'I'm not the heavy lover type.'" [15]

Jackie, for her part, avidly pursued Jack, but few of her friends were convinced that passion played much of a part in her considerations. Jack Kennedy was wealthy beyond her dreams. (However, she did not inherit much upon his death.) He also reminded her of her beloved papa, the dashing and romantic "Black Jack" Bouvier, with whom Jack Kennedy indeed had much in common—including their unstoppable philandering. And Jack was glamorous, witty, and fun—he was one of those people who could make you feel as if you were the meaning and center of the entire world, so long as he was with you. And, though he was young himself—only thirty-six at the time of the wedding—he was still twelve years older than she. (Throughout her life Jackie, who loathed politics and disdained power as such, was attracted to wealthy, magnetic, older men.) For her, too, it seemed a perfect match, and the wedding took place in September 1953. It was one of the biggest social events of the year.

Yet trouble always loomed. Jack's back problems were devastating him; he had to hobble around on crutches much of the time. He also suffered from Addison's disease, a rare and progressive hormonal deficiency that began to exacerbate the troubles with his back; in 1955 he finally submitted to an operation. It was a re-

> Throughout her life Jackie, who loathed politics and disdained power as such, was attracted to wealthy, magnetic, older men.

sounding failure and Jack almost died. His family was summoned for the administration of the last rites, but then he made a dramatic recovery, underwent a more successful operation, and spent the next several months in traction. During this period he added even greater luster to his name by "writing" *Profiles in Courage,* a study of eight American senators who had taken brave stands in the face of furious opposition, not only from their colleagues but also—more perilously—from their constituents. The book was published in 1956, and the following year it won the Pulitzer Prize for Biography against stiff opposition. (*Profiles* has remained fodder for controversy ever since. It is generally accepted now that

(opposite) Jackie and Jack on their wedding day, September 1953

Jack, on crutches before back surgery, and Jackie, 1954

Jack at the 1956 Democratic National Convention

though the organization and overall idea of the book may have been Kennedy's, the actual writing was not; and that he won the Pulitzer because his father, and even more so Joe's close friend, Arthur Krock, who was a member of the Pulitzer committee, bull-dozed the award through.[16] (Once again the Kennedy myth and the Kennedy reality hopelessly diverge.)

All this was central to his run for the main prize, the presidency, in 1960, and by then Jack's image was fixed. He was the prophet of youth, vigor, freshness, and change; the Republicans, as symbol-

ized by Dwight David Eisenhower (who had been president for
eight years and was not running for reelection), were old, sclerotic,
and tired. They seemed perpetually moribund and gray; Kennedy
burst on the scene in bold and glorious colors:

> Soldier, scholar, horseman, he,
>
> And all he did done perfectly
>
> As though he had but that one trade alone. [17]

All that Kennedy symbolized eventually came to be known as
Camelot.

*Jack and Jackie with John Jr.
after the baby's christening,
December 1960*

BOUVIER

The greatest influence on Jackie's life was her father, "Black Jack" Bouvier, so called because of his swarthy good looks (to be found again in her son, John Jr.) and his notorious reputation as a man of sharp practice and dubious morals. He was so steeped in womanizing that he conducted an affair with another "gorgeous creature" during his honeymoon—on board a ship! (Jackie loved telling this story.) He even had the audacity to be photographed with his wife while holding another woman's hand. His wife, Janet, came to detest him bitterly; their eventual divorce was acrimonious and ugly.

It also wounded young Jackie and her sister, Lee, because they idolized their father, who was charismatic, adoring, and attentive, and made them feel like princesses. Jackie forgave him every fault, as he, indeed, forgave her, and he set the pattern for her ideal man: He was certainly in many ways an older version of Jack. (Though Jack did not cheat on his honeymoon, nor was he an alcoholic. Indeed, because of a bad stomach he could not drink at all, and despite the tendency of many Kennedys to overindulge, he was a virtual teetotaler.)

Not everyone was so understanding of Black Jack. Janet's father loathed him so profoundly that after the divorce, he cut Jackie and Lee out of his will and forced them to sign papers agreeing to the disinheritance. (This is why the daughters of the wealthy Bouviers were relatively "poor" themselves.) The night before Black Jack was scheduled to give Jackie away at her wedding, he got blind, stinking drunk and could not even stand the following morning. Hugh Auchincloss, Jackie's stepfather, did the honors instead.

Black Jack continued to swashbuckle right and left, always with great style and flair, and eventually he ran through his fortune. He drank continually and died of liver cancer in 1957 at the age of sixty-six. His last word, apparently, was "Jackie."

But Black Jack was a consummate Bouvier and had style. Jackie inherited that style in spades. "It takes a lot of civilization gone just a little high to make a wit," wrote Gore Vidal, who is related to Jackie, and the Bouviers had civilization; the Kennedys, by contrast, did not. They were rich, they were dynamic, they were (or at least the patriarch was) ambitious—but they were still *arriviste* peasants: In comparison to the cultivated (French) Bouviers, they had just gotten off the boat.

John "Black Jack" Bouvier, Virginia Kernochan, and Janet Bouvier in Tuxedo Park, New York, June 1934

Jackie was appalled by the Kennedy family when she met them: the roughhousing, the obsession with football and other violent sports, the savage competition, the endless mockery of one another and (with even greater gusto) of everyone else, and the general hostility displayed to everyone who had not been born a Kennedy, which included her.

She did like Joe Sr., who in turn was charmed by her and was one of the few to appreciate her merits, and she came to adore both Bobby and Ted, though the sisters were horrors as far as she was concerned: uncouth, ill-mannered, barbarian. She was interested in books, music, and ballet; they cared only about politics, power, and sports. She called them the Rah-Rah Girls; they ragged her cultivated interests and her sugary "babykins" voice. Never did the two camps come to terms, and after Jack's assassination the sisters would gladly have seen her gone. Had it not been for the intervention of Bobby and Ted, they might have succeeded.

However, this was all very private; publicly there was only harmony, unity, and smiles. They played touch football games at

Jackie and Black Jack at the Southampton Horse Show on Long Island, New York, August 1934

"Black Jack"

Jackie leads her pony after competing at the Southampton Horse Show, August 1934

Hyannis Port and America was charmed; they were active and photogenic and America was dazed. They did everything together: They even governed as one. Jack's brothers, especially Bobby, helped organize his campaigns and Bobby also became attorney general. This raised eyebrows among some, but others were thrilled. Many of us grew up in families in which siblings bickered constantly and even hated one another, but the Kennedys played games together, laughed, wrote books, married film stars, loved one another, and always got together for important occasions. And we saw it all on national television.

It was delirious and intoxicating—"You go to my head," as Frank Sinatra, a good buddy of Jack's, so memorably sang—and Jackie was an integral part of it: Americans seized upon her as their very own sweetheart. She was a rich girl who worked, a debutante who was not a snob, a glittering adornment—far more than an adornment, indeed—who at times even outshone her husband,

Jackie (third from left) sets sail to spend her junior year of college in France, 1949

the comet becoming a star. Kennedy later, on his state visit to France (where Jackie, who spoke fluent French, interpreted for him and Charles De Gaulle), famously remarked: "I am the man who accompanied Jacqueline Kennedy to Paris, and I have enjoyed it."

Everyone enjoyed it; it only took a little time. Jackie was the personification of style, by far the most stylish woman to adorn the White House in this century. She was so stylish, in fact, that Americans were put off by her at first: Her fashions were too foreign, too French, too superior to what her countrymen were used to. By 1960, however, when the young and beautiful Jackie was campaigning for the young and handsome Jack, the public had been completely won over. Jackie was so much the fashion setter that it

Bobby and Jack in Jack's senate office, August 1959

The First Family leaving Easter service in Palm Beach, Florida, 1962

would be almost like having Audrey Hepburn in the White House, and that provided a simply staggering contrast to Ike and Mamie Eisenhower or even to Richard and Pat Nixon. "You go to my head" indeed. When the Bouvier style combined with the Kennedy magnetism, it produced two children. It also produced Camelot.

CAMELOT

But what *was* Camelot (so named by his widow after the assassination, who likened her fallen husband and his court to the musical about the King Arthur legend currently playing on Broadway)?

Why was it so important, and why did it enthrall the country as it did for three years? As much as anything else it was a contrast with the Eisenhower era, which had supposedly deadened and stultified the American will, purpose, and creativity. Camelot was a style.

The ultimate legacy of Camelot is that it swept in a new *spirit*, a boldness, a lightness—that particular Kennedy magic, which only Jack and Jackie truly seemed to possess (and which they passed on to John). Regardless of what JFK, as he was so affectionately known, did or did not do as president, he made people—Americans above all, but Europeans and South Americans and Asians as well—feel good about themselves. Everything seemed possible, even if very little happened in fact. Kennedy was more responsible for the buildup of the Vietnam War than his successor, Lyndon Johnson, and Johnson was more responsible for advances in civil rights than Kennedy, but that is not the perception: How could an "oaf" like Johnson possibly compete with Kennedy's golden light? Kennedy could do no wrong (and men like Johnson and Nixon, by extension, could do no right); and the most commonly voiced plaint in the years immediately following his assassination was, "If only he had lived," "If only Jack were around there would have been no Vietnam," "If only Jack were here, America would be all right again." It was never "all right" during his administration, but people thought it was; Kennedy did little as president and yet he seemed to do everything. Voters were so entranced by him that they took the promise for the deed.

John Fitzgerald Kennedy announced a new dawn on the horizon and people saw it; he announced that the torch had been passed and people felt the flame. Richard Nixon was more experienced, in certain ways more intelligent, and in some respects better equipped to be president (though he was also more tortured, insecure, and riven with the hatreds and paranoia that eventually destroyed him), but he could never have announced a new dawn, could never have inspired a Camelot of any sort, because Nixon had no style.

A telling incident: Almost everyone agrees that the turning point for Jack was his famous first debate with Nixon when both were running for president in 1960. The debate was televised, and viewers saw one man who was devilishly handsome, jaunty, at ease, and fresh looking, and another who was dark, jowly, nervous, and sweaty. Kennedy overwhelmingly "won" the debate—according to those who saw it. According to those who heard it on the

Background photo: Caroline, Jackie, and John Jr. in Virginia, November, 1962

radio, however—who listened to what the candidates said and had no idea how the candidates looked—Nixon won. Did style really win out over substance? Or did viewers, who were able to judge style as well as content, in fact make the truer choice? Image may not be everything, but it counts for a great deal—perhaps in politics above all. So when John Fitzgerald Kennedy was murdered in Dallas on November 22, 1963, the light seemed to go out of the country. And that was not merely from the death of style.

The war in Vietnam escalated and the country was polarized; father was pitched against son and a new Civil War seemed to be brewing. "For arrogance and hatred are the wares/Peddled in the thoroughfares," wrote Yeats about similar troubles decades before in another country.[18] Kennedy's successor was despised; Kennedy's brother Bobby was assassinated, as was Martin Luther King Jr., and the country was in despair. Then the next great hope, Ted Kennedy, was involved in the death of Mary Jo Kopechne at Chappaquiddick. There seemed to be no end to the grief.

Jack and John Jr. in Newport, Rhode Island, September 1963

Jackie, returning from a vacation, is greeted by Caroline, John Jr., and her husband, October 1963

Jack, Caroline, and John Jr. in the Oval Office, October 1962

Jack and John Jr. in the
Oval Office, October 1963

Since then we have recovered, but the Kennedy line may have been irreparably damaged. We seem worlds away now from the peaceful time of an *Esquire* cover that neatly plotted the possible (expected) reign: JFK, president from 1960 to 1968; RFK, president from 1968 to 1976; EMK (Ted), president from 1976 to 1984; and then? John Fitzgerald Kennedy Jr. could have followed, but not until 1996 at least—which now, of course, is here; but it was a sign of the Kennedy mania sweeping the country at the time that the boy was being seriously proposed as president while he was still wearing diapers.

Instead we have had two assassinations, the Chappaquiddick mess, divorces, more drug and sex scandals than daytime television can encompass, one girl paralyzed,[19] one death from a drug overdose,[20] one alleged rape,[21] and who knows how many other incidents that never made it to public view. The Kennedys, once the most glittering family in America and our apparently predestined leaders, are now a morass, by and large, although there are exceptions. Many citizens look to John Fitzgerald Kennedy Jr. as the family's last hope. He is, after all, the perfect candidate (like his father): the son of the president who was the country's brightest star; the Prince whose birth coincided with his father's election and the beginning of the Camelot dream; the Redeemer, the Man Who Would Be King, if only he wanted it.

Yet nobody knows whether he wants it or not, including John himself.

John is escorted by a Secret Service agent during a Memorial Day service, May 1963

Jack and Richard Nixon, presidential candidates, before their first televised debate, September 1960

WHITE HOUSE DAYS

JOHN FITZGERALD KENNEDY JR. was "a dream baby who laughed all the time but already seemed to have a will of his own," [22] and nothing could control his exuberance. Although he was often docile and obedient, he was just as frequently willful and overexcited; presidents, prime ministers, and empresses walked in stately procession through the White House, but if they displeased him or if he was simply in a riotous humor, he would yell and kick his heels, and no one, not even his revered father, could do much—or anything—to stop him.

JFK, who had received thousands of orders but rarely, if ever, any love from his parents, was a doting, tremendously affectionate father, but even he at times worried about John. One day on the White House balcony, John, exuberantly cheered at a parade passing below him (he was always in love with pageantry and uni-

forms) and played with his toy six-shooters. One of them fell out of his belt and almost landed on the head of his father's state guest—President Josip Broz Tito of Yugoslavia. The elder Kennedy was not amused.

More often, however, the president delighted in John's and Caroline's presence. He gave them the run of the White House, and every morning he let them walk to his office to play for ten minutes (John's favorite hiding place was behind the sliding panel in front of his father's desk, which had once belonged to Franklin Roosevelt); then they would go off with their governess. Occasionally John stayed longer when his elder sister was in nursery school, and the president always found it difficult to say goodbye.

He seemed to find it just as difficult to say no. Visiting dignitaries often looked askance

(above) John explores the Oval Office, May 1962

(opposite) Jack and John Jr. greeting visitors at the White House, October 1963

65

John Jr., held by his godmother Mrs. Charles L. Bartlett, at his christening, December 1960

"a dream baby who laughed all the time but already seemed to have a will of his own..."

when Kennedy, in the midst of official discussions in the Oval Office, suddenly grinned as his children entered. He would break off his talks, tickle them, play hide-and-seek, and delight in their presence as any father would. This father happened to be the president of the United States, but that never seemed to matter to him as much as playing with Caroline and John.

He loved to tell them fairy tales and make up stories and to watch films with them in the White House projection room, where he had a popcorn machine installed; even in the midst of the Cuban Missile Crisis, he took time out to carve them a jack-o'-lantern. His bad back often got in the way of his frolics, but even that wouldn't blunt his enthusiasm. At one lunch time, when John could not be found, his governess, Maud Shaw, had a pretty good idea of where to find him: in the helicopter hangar. According to her:

Sure enough, he was [there]. And so was the President. Both of them were sitting at the controls of the helicopter with flying helmets on. The President was playing the game seriously with his son, taking orders from Flight Captain John, thoroughly absorbed in the whole thing. I retreated quietly and left father and son very happy together. [23]

Although many such scenes took place in private, visitors who witnessed the closeness between father and son were often charmed.

Jackie Kennedy was as stern a parent as her husband was gushing. If the latter had had his way, the children would have been hopelessly spoiled, so Jackie went to the opposite extreme. She was

Jack and John Jr. in the Oval Office, October 1963

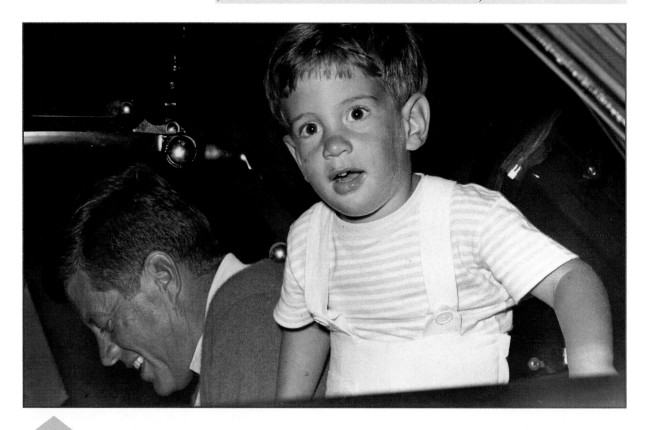

John Jr. makes his father laugh by announcing, "Daddy, I think they're trying to take my picture," August 1963

never mean or cruel and John and Caroline adored her, but she insisted that they be raised with manners, discipline, and the kind of control that proved, years later, to be so lamentably lacking in many of their cousins.

Occasionally this led to a certain cheapness. Jackie Kennedy, who had felt somewhat "poor" throughout her life, did not always spend money lavishly even while living in the White House, at least not on others (she made up for this self-control with a vengeance after she married Aristotle Onassis), and her children were never showered with gifts at Christmas or birthdays (celebrated jointly, for they were born three years and two days apart). She also had a knack for spoiling the sport. The president may have loved movies and may have loved watching them with Caroline and John, but Jackie insisted that the children be in bed by 8:00 P.M. sharp. This rule was immutable, so no matter what was happening or what the film was—even if the dénouement lurked only five minutes away—off they would have to trot. What Jack thought of this is not entirely clear. It must be noted, however, that the children did not seem to feel deprived; and to Jackie this forced "austerity" was very important.

The Kennedy women disliked Jackie and she disliked them in return. She was also well aware of the ruthlessness in too many of the Kennedy men (including Bobby, with whom she was very close), so she insisted that her children be as little "Kennedy" as possible. Despite the fact that Caroline and her grandmother Rose were intimate, Jackie seems largely to have succeeded. Certainly John and his sister have maintained a dignified low profile throughout most of their lives. If it were not for the fact that reporters hound them without mercy and invent stories where there are none, they would rarely make the papers at all.

Jackie shielded them from those reporters and from greedy onlookers as best she could (though this was to some extent a los-

John Jr. attempts to board the presidential plane, June 1963

Jackie introduces John to Empress Farah, wife of the Shah of Iran, April 1962

ing battle) and even from the loftiness of the White House. "I want my children to be brought up in more personal surroundings, not in the state rooms," she told the chief usher, J. B. West. "And I don't want them to be raised by nurses and Secret Service agents."[24] There was also the famous fight over the White House *Guidebook* that was being prepared. George F. Mobley, a staff photographer for *National Geographic,* had taken a picture of John and Caroline playing in John's bedroom. Everyone lobbied feverishly to include it in the book, but Jackie was firmly opposed. "Gentlemen," she said imperiously, "even at the age of two one's bedroom should be private." The picture did not appear.

And yet there were contradictions, as always with this curious woman. Although she supervised John and Caroline's upbringing, it was their governess, Maud Shaw, an Englishwoman, who raised

John inspects Captain Cecil Stoughton's camera, November 1963. Stoughton was the official White House photographer.

them. She bathed them and Jackie watched; she inculcated "British" manners and Jackie approved. Miss Shaw was rightfully proud of her handiwork, and Jackie certainly deserves recognition for bringing her on board. But she has probably received too much of the credit that rightfully belongs to Miss Shaw; and Jackie was not always the saintly mother the publicity machine has depicted:

> She left Caroline and John-John for long periods of time. She insisted they stay in Palm Beach when she moved into the White House, saying she could not cope with settling them in while she had so much unpacking to do. When they came to Washington the next month, she left them with their nannies while she took off to New York to shop, to Virginia to go fox-hunting, and to Palm Beach to relax.[25]

Still there is no denying that her children were well-bred. They were schooled diligently by Jackie and Miss Shaw in politeness and good manners, and to this day people are astonished at how unpretentious John in particular is. They expect a snob and find a

John travels with Maud Shaw to Andrews Air Force Base to see his father off on a trip, May 1963

man who casually shoots the breeze with construction workers. They expect a monster of self-absorption and find a regular guy. The only time he was difficult as a child was when his effervescent personality took over—which, alas, it frequently did.

John was hyperactive; he had enormous difficulty concentrating or even sitting still for more than a few minutes at a time. He was "noted for his singing, dancing, and high-octane curiosity," [26]

Jackie and John at the White House, May 1963. Eunice Kennedy Shriver and her daughter, Maria, are behind Jackie and John.

Jack and John Jr. at the White House, October 1963

and this theatrical restlessness bore fruit years later when he turned to acting as a release—and an escape. His boisterousness eventually became a problem at school, and John, despite his evident intelligence, was never a good student at any level.

But he was an entertainer. After his father's murder, he used to cheer up his mother and sister with his outrageous imitations of the Beatles. And John was naturally upbeat. He was also, in one sense, lucky that he was too young at three years to have understood or even, in a certain way, experienced the disruptions and tragedy that dogged his family and him.

Caroline was not as fortunate; she felt uprooted and unhappy during her first several months in the White House. Jackie, in a brief recollection, made a haunting reference to "this sad little face," although the three-year-old eventually adapted and undeniably shared many happy moments as First Girl. She adored her little brother and insisted that only her comb and brush be used on his hair; Miss Shaw was surprised to see how little jealousy or sibling rivalry existed between them. They were proud of and pleased with each other, and on November 22, 1963, the two of them were happily playing together and talking eagerly about their upcoming birthdays when the shots rang out in Dallas.

It was Bobby who broke the news to John, but he was too young to know what it meant. Caroline was not—she was six— and the miserable task of informing her devolved upon the governess. The little girl was shattered; she wept so copiously that Miss Shaw was afraid she might choke. At the funeral she desperately clutched the hand of Bob Foster, a Secret Service agent (John later became so close to Foster that he occasionally called him "Daddy," until Jackie had Foster reassigned), and for months afterward Caroline was listless and depressed. Her uncle Bobby noted that she no longer let anyone get close to her; and although he, despite his own debilitating grief, did all he could to elevate her spirits and become to John and Caroline the father they had lost, she remained haunted for years by the event. And less than five years later, of course, this "new" father was murdered as well.

To John, ignorance was bliss. One of the most unforgettable images of the last thirty-five years took place at JFK's funeral: With the passing of the caisson, which had once carried the body of Franklin Delano Roosevelt and now bore the body of John Fitzgerald Kennedy, John Jr., in his bright blue coat, stepped away from his mother and saluted. It was at once wrenching and utterly charming, and a grieving nation wept. Yet the boy, who had always loved guns, uniforms, pageantry, and parades, was responding to the glory of the moment, not to its tragedy. He did

John in the Cabinet Room, October 1963

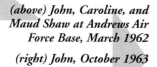

(above) John, Caroline, and Maud Shaw at Andrews Air Force Base, March 1962

(right) John, October 1963

not comprehend what was passing, and today he confesses that he cannot in truth remember the occasion.[27]

How could he? He was celebrating his third birthday. Later that night John marched about briskly at his birthday "party," which was more a wake than a celebration to most of its numbed participants. The adults found it difficult to watch without breaking into tears anew. Caroline gravely looked on.

John's famous salute, November 1963

LIKE FATHER, LIKE SON

JACK AND JOHN JR. WERE TOgether almost continually in the days leading up to the assassination (the helicopter incident took place only a few days before), and already numerous similarities were becoming apparent. More appeared in time.

Both were polite and in many respects perfect gentlemen (so long as John's exuberance was held in check); both were fond of the sea. (This also helped draw John close to Aristotle Onassis, with whom he had a more congenial relationship than most people realize.) Both loved uniforms and celebrations; yet both, despite this, were surprisingly slovenly.

This may come as a shock to those who have seen the thousands of photographs in which Jack is looking spruce and dapper and every inch the polished politician; but though he did look smashing in white tie and tails (in truth this elegant man looked smashing in anything), he "was usually nonchalant about his personal appearance, frequently showing up in rumpled suits, frayed shirts, and mismatched socks."[28] To be sure, this was before he met Jackie.

And John Jr., he of the dynamite tuxedos and finely pin-striped shirts? Hopeless, and for many years beyond repair. Indeed, for many years his mother, one of the great clotheshorses of the twentieth century, despaired of him. She would appear for lunch dressed to the nines; John would drag himself in dressed to the ones. "A typical outfit included shorts with boxers hanging well below the hem, a frayed Brooks Brothers button-down shirt,

(above) Jack and John Jr. leaving Hyannis Port in a helicopter, September 1963

(opposite) Jack and John Jr. at the Rose Garden entrance of the Oval Office, October 1963

Both loved jokes and stories, especially Irish ones . . .

John Jr. and Jack on Veterans' Day, November 1963

and Top-Siders"[29]—and this was on a good day. It was not as if he could not afford a new Brooks Brothers shirt or a pair of shorts that covered his underwear. John was making a *statement.* And he meant it to sting, by Jove.

Other shared traits appeared over the years. Jack Kennedy, Pulitzer Prize–winning author and thirty-fifth president of the United States, was an atrocious speller throughout his life; so, it quickly became apparent, was John.

Both loved jokes and stories, especially Irish ones, and it was part of John's theatrical nature to tell them in a variety of authentic accents. This is an interesting trait, since the Kennedys, especially Joe Sr., were as adept at playing down their Irishness as they were at playing it up. (One of the chapters of Garry Wills's brilliant study is entitled "Semi-Irish," and Wills points out that "six of Joseph Kennedy's children married—not one to an Irish spouse. They had not been brought up to respect their own."[30]) John, however, eagerly embraced Irish theater—he even played the lead in John Millington Synge's *The Playboy of the Western World* at Brown University and made his professional acting debut in Brian Friel's *Winners* at the Irish Arts Center in Manhattan— and he has a tattoo of a shamrock on his arm. The patriarch would no doubt have been appalled.

John also shared his father's passion for football, although that may be a general Kennedy trait; and both were very proud of their bodies. (John, indeed, is an outright exhibitionist, as we shall see a little later.) And neither of them could ever tolerate being bored. JFK actually introduced a form of crisis management into the White House (the Cuban Missile Crisis was its most extreme manifestation) in order to keep from dying of boredom;[31] John Jr. was so hyperactive that at one point in his adolescence Jackie actually sent him to a psychiatrist. The sessions had little effect.

Both Jack and John were ghastly about money. They were not cheap, but thoroughly cavalier. They never carried cash or never carried enough, borrowed constantly from friends (not all of whom were millionaires by any stretch of the imagination) and often forgot to pay it back; or wouldn't pay it back for months; or would pay it back only if pestered about it; and they drove their friends and retainers crazy. "The notion of working at a job as if your life depended on it fascinated [John]," according to his

On the beach at Hyannis Port, January 1995

Brown classmate Christa de Souza,[32] but somehow few were or are irritated, and most are only charmed. (Indeed, one sidelight upon the practice is that when John does get around to writing checks in reimbursement, the recipients don't always cash them: They would rather hang on to the signature and the piece of paper!)

Father and son shared that magic, that special grace, that glow or electricity that lights up a room the minute they enter; and this is one of the most fundamental ingredients to the final and most notorious link of all: Both of them were incessant womanizers. They even had a penchant—though by no means an exclusive one—for actresses. This theme will be elucidated more fully later, but there is one major difference in their attitudes. John can be gallant and tender with women, though he also can be thoughtless and cruel, whereas Jack saw women purely as conquests and would frequently bed them once only and then move on. Nevertheless the appetite and the charisma were there. Like father, like son indeed.

John lights up the room with Mikhail and Raïsa Gorbachev at the JFK Library, 1992

Father and son shared that magic, that special grace, that glow or electricity that lights up a room the minute they enter...

John skating in New York City, May 1994

IN NEW YORK

AFTER THE TRAGEDY

Following the assassination that shocked the nation and destroyed this Kennedy family, Jackie and her children were marked. They had to move out of the White House, of course, because President Johnson and his family were now the rightful occupants, but in their dwelling at 3017 N Street in Washington, D.C., they were virtual prisoners. Sympathetic well-wishers and morbid gawkers alike made their lives intolerable, and the police had to erect barricades and block off roads just to keep the rubberneckers away. People stared at them if they did not keep their curtains drawn; photographers hovered about incessantly in hopes of getting a shot. Jackie could not bear it, nor could she tolerate the kindness of the Johnsons, whom she sneered at behind their backs as uncouth buffoons. This, it must be noted, was a typical attitude not only of the Kennedys but also of their hangers-on:

> On the evening of his return from Dallas, the new President, arriving at his EOB office, asked an aide to get him two pieces of presidential stationery. The assistant went to the nearby room of a Kennedy aide, who handed over the sheets with eyes flashing. "The body not cold yet—and he's grabbing for the President's stationery." Lyndon Johnson wanted the paper so that his first letters as President of the United States would be handwritten notes to Caroline and John Kennedy Jr. [33]

Eventually Jackie fled the nation's capital with her children: Less than a year after the

(above) Jackie and the children leave the White House, December 1963

(opposite) Captain Dave Buckley holds John at the New York World's Fair, September 1964

John meets Mickey Mouse at the New York World's Fair, April 1965

Background photo: The apartment building at 1040 Fifth Avenue

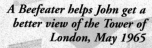

A Beefeater helps John get a better view of the Tower of London, May 1965

murder she purchased a $200,000 fifteen-room cooperative apartment in New York City at 1040 Fifth Avenue. Mrs. Kennedy spent another $125,000 to refurbish it. Most of Jack Kennedy's millions had gone to his children upon his death, but although Jackie received only $25,000, plus half of all his property and belongings, she was obviously not poor. Among other things, she received a subsistence both from the government (as the widow of a slain president) and from the Kennedy family.

Coincidentally, Bobby also moved to New York and ran (successfully) for senator from that state the same year. The Kennedys have occasionally been accused of carpetbagging, but the fact is that despite their Bostonian origins, they were never particularly tied to that city or any other. Their one loyalty has always been to themselves alone, and they have moved freely from Maine to Florida to Massachusetts to Washington to California to New York City and back again. John Jr., for example, has no regional accent, and many people are surprised at this. They shouldn't be. He spent the first three years of his life in D.C., spent the next thirteen in Manhattan, and then attended schools in Massachusetts and Rhode Island. Geographically he is a New Yorker, and has spent most of his time in that city since graduating from Brown University in 1983.

Life in New York was a step up, and although there were mounds of reporters and curiosity seekers hounding the family almost daily, they still seemed manageable compared to the army that had crushed them in D.C. Jackie actually found it possible to stroll through Central Park with her children from time to time without being recognized—or at least pestered. This would have been inconceivable along the Potomac. And she had always despised politics in any case, even when she occupied the White House ("I can't understand it," her husband used to say. "She breathes all the political gases that flow around us but she never seems to inhale them"[34]), so New York, with its arts and letters and society and cosmopolitan ambiance, was very much her kind of town.

St. David's School

In February 1965, John began classes at St. David's School in Manhattan, a Catholic institution founded in 1951. His first day was eventful: He punched a fellow student in the nose.

John was popular with his teachers and mixed well with other students, fisticuffs notwithstanding. His best friend at St. David's was his cousin Willie (William Kennedy Smith), with whom he has always remained very tight. But he made friends

John meets Queen Elizabeth in London as Jackie and Caroline look on, May 1965

John and Caroline enjoy a scooter boat ride in Regent's Park, London, May 1965

easily (too easily, as far as his mother was concerned; John talked to anyone, including reporters, whom Jackie loathed above all other forms of human or nonhuman life), and he seemed happy there.

In May of that year the Kennedys traveled to London with Miss Shaw—who did not make the return trip. She had decided to retire to her native country, but John and Caroline were not informed of this until after their return to New York. Once again they adjusted well. They achieved a good deal of practice in losing people over the years.

While in London the children were presented to Queen Elizabeth, but John was much more impressed by the Changing of the Guard at Buckingham Palace, the cannons at the Tower of London, and the various parades he witnessed. Naturally, the British press hounded the family throughout the entire visit.

Back in New York, John played almost daily in Central Park and became increasingly interested in sports, which remain a passion—especially football, baseball, and boxing. (But not horses. He was allergic to them, yet his mother insisted that he ride despite this because *she* liked riding. John made the best of it.) Jackie even had him taught boxing by the Secret Service so he could protect himself against cruel schoolmates who used to taunt him about his dead father and because she was afraid he might become a sissy.

The Secret Service was everywhere: It was the agency's job to shadow the Kennedys twenty-four hours a day. Already there were death threats, and even the intrusive spectators to whom no one's

Background photo: St. David's School

John and astronaut John Glenn, May 1967

A friend comforts John after he hurt himself playing at a family wedding, August 1966

privacy was sacred could become troublesome. The agents were discreet, at least at times, but they were always present—even at Halloween. Eventually John became adept at evading them.

But not even the Secret Service could forestall every indignity—especially not when the world's press was involved. Jackie loved to ski, so on a 1966 ski trip she was teaching Caroline the rudiments of the sport when two photographers began jostling for position and knocked the little girl down. How do you explain such a thing to an eight-year-old? Jackie asked bitterly, but the press never seemed to wonder. It certainly did not care. When John was still in diapers he had crawled up and down the aisle of Air Force One to the delight of the press corps. At age three he had glared at reporters and cried out, "What are those silly people taking my picture for?" A few years later he had fired a water pistol at the face of a pesky photographer. None of this had discouraged the constant attention of the press.

In 1967 John, Jackie, and Caroline made their first trip to Ireland. They landed on the front pages every day of the month-long visit. Nowhere were they safe or immune. And it only grew worse with coming events.

> The Secret Service was everywhere: It was the agency's job to shadow the Kennedys twenty-four hours a day.

Bobby, his daughter Kathleen, and John ski in Aspen, Colorado, December 1964

UNCLE BOBBY

Bobby Kennedy, who was now the junior senator from New York, was very close to his late brother's family and used to talk to his niece and nephew about the world's social problems. They were deeply affected. As their mother noted:

There's so much else in the world, outside this sanctuary we live in. Bobby has told them about some of those things—the children of Harlem, for instance. He told them about the rats and about the terrible living conditions that exist right here in the midst of a rich city. Broken windows letting in the cold. John was so touched by that he said he'd go to work and use the money he made to put windows in those houses. The children rounded up their best toys last Christmas and gave them away.[35]

Bobby, one of the few Kennedys who liked Jackie (Ted was another), and who adored his niece and nephew, had become a father figure to Caroline and John, and he made every effort to include them in his own family's gatherings—which his wife, Ethel, resented. (She was actually more Kennedy than the Kennedys, more like one of the sisters than the sisters themselves, and she may be the only outsider who was ever truly accepted and embraced by the clan—though even this is doubtful and she was fairly well ignored by the Kennedys after her husband's assassination.) Indeed, according to biographer Kitty Kelley, Bobby "spent more time with his sister-in-law and her children than his own, and Jackie leaned on him for everything." Kelley goes further still:

> She even considered at one point asking him to adopt Caroline and John-John, feeling she could never raise them by herself, but Bobby told her the idea was crazy, that she had to go on. He gave as much as he could at the time, offering her all his love and support and protection.[36]

Jackie in turn campaigned feverishly for her brother-in-law during his senatorial campaign and even allowed John and Caroline to appear. This was all but unheard-of for so protective and apolitical a mother.

Bobby's ruthlessness had become far less savage over the years, and although he once had been a right-wing hatchetman for Joe McCarthy and then a pragmatic pit bull for his brother, he seemed genuinely to have mellowed as a man and grown tremendously as a politician in the five years since his brother's death. Jack had always been a centrist, but Bobby was becoming something akin to a genuine radical, at least in certain respects. However, on June 6, 1968, on the eve of what might have proved to be a historic run for the presidency, he was gunned down in the kitchen of a Los Angeles hotel. He did not actually die until the following day.

John at Bobby's campaign office in New York City, September 1964

Background photo: John and Caroline at Bobby's funeral at St. Patrick's Cathedral in New York City, June 1968

THE ONASSIS YEARS

JACKIE AND ARI

Jackie Kennedy was unquestionably the most famous woman in the world; for seven or eight years, since the inauguration of JFK, she had also been the most admired. That all changed with the murder of Bobby Kennedy and her subsequent marriage to Aristotle Onassis.

She had known Onassis for years; her sister, Lee, had had an affair with him and at one point was hoping to marry him. In August 1963 Jackie had given premature birth (by Caesarean section, the same way John had been delivered) to a second son, Patrick Bouvier Kennedy, but two days later Patrick died of a lung infection. The president and his wife were shattered and Aristotle Onassis offered to put his opulent yacht, the *Christina*, at Jackie and Lee's disposal, to sail wherever and

with whomever they desired. Jackie gratefully accepted his gracious offer, although Jack and Bobby were suspicious of this divorced billionaire Greek jetsetter. Onassis quickly lost interest in Lee and was much more taken with her beguiling older sister.

A few months later, after Jack's assassination, Onassis accompanied Lee and her husband to Washington for the funeral; he was one of the few guests invited to stay in the White House. Eventually he and Jackie began a discreet affair, in New York, in Paris, and perhaps on the yacht, and by May 1968 it was obvious to the incensed Kennedys (even though many of them detested her, they expected her to remain a lifelong widow/martyr) that she was planning to remarry. Onassis had a far shrewder grasp of her than any of them could provide:

(above) John, Caroline, and Jackie head to Switzerland for a ski vacation, January 1966

(opposite) John at the World Series with Caroline, Jackie, and Aristotle, October 1969

here any more. If they're killing Kennedys, my kids are number-one targets. . . . I want to get out." Four months later, she flew to Greece and married for a second time.

ARISTOTLE ONASSIS AND JOHN

Onassis worked diligently to win over Jackie's daughter and son. Even during the earliest stages of the affair he brought costly presents for both; and once he began courting their mother in earnest he showered them with gifts, took John fishing, or to baseball games, swam with him, and talked to him about their shared love of the sea. After the wedding he became even more generous: a speedboat for John, a sailboat for Caroline, jukeboxes, mini-Jeeps, Shetland ponies. (Jackie, who had always insisted on moderation, let him spoil the two outrageously.) And there was more, according to Onassis's friend Costa Gratsos:

> But beyond presents, he tried to give of himself, to be with them. He attended their school plays in New York and went out to Jackie's place in New Jersey to watch them ride. And the truth is, Ari hated it there. He didn't care for horses at all. But he'd go out anyway, when he was in New York, and most of the time he'd just stand around. He was always complaining that the mud and the horse dung ruined his shoes and pants.[40]

Onassis made every attempt to become one of the family, yet it was difficult and no one among the Kennedys, including Jackie, attempted to meet him even halfway. The wedding, the yacht, the island, the Greek Orthodox ritual, the circus that this tremendously ballyhooed wedding inevitably became, with photographers actually falling off rooftops into the sea—all this was strange to John. He and his sister were gloomy presences at the ceremony, but their lives were cushioned as much as possible. They continued to live and attend school in New York throughout the academic year, and they were surrounded by familiar friends and family and even Secret Service agents.

However, inevitably the oddity of the arrangement took its toll. Onassis was fabulously generous, but he showed up in the New

Background photo: Jackie, Caroline, and John visit Jack's grave, June 1968

York apartment only from time to time and often seemed a stranger. John called him "Mr. Onassis," not "Ari"; and in the end, although he grew very fond of Onassis, he looked upon him more as a grandfather than as a father figure. In addition, whatever relationship they did have became decidedly strained when Onassis resumed his affair with Maria Callas, which Jackie bitterly resented. Yet no one was more responsible for that than Jackie herself.

JACKIE $$$

Jackie's attitude toward Onassis was fantastically mercenary from the beginning (when it took weeks to hammer out a prenuptial agreement designed more to make her wealthy than to protect

Ten-year-old John takes a jump at the Somerset Hills Pony Club in New Jersey, May 1971

John with Jackie and Aristotle in New York City, February 1969

John and Jackie in Greece,
August 1969

him against predation) to the end (when Jackie took Onassis's relatives to court to receive a larger sum upon his death). Onassis, when he learned how comparatively little she received from the Kennedys, called her a political prisoner. He ended up ransoming her in grand style:

> Onassis agreed to pay her $3 million outright, which could either be deposited in her bank account or used to buy non-taxable bonds, plus the annual interest on a $1 million trust fund for each of her children until they reached the age of 21. In the event of a divorce or (his) death, Jackie would receive an additional $200,000 per year for life. In return she would relinquish her hereditary rights, which under Greek law meant she surrendered her claim to a maximum of one-fourth of her husband's estate.[41]

John and Jackie bike through Central Park, November 1970

"If I paid any more this would cease to be a marriage and become an acquisition," Onassis is famous for saying, but that is exactly what it was—and this acquisition kept costing him a fortune. (In the end it was Jackie, not he, who reneged on the terms so scrupulously arranged.)

Jackie was given an allowance of $30,000 a month, which she found routinely impossible to survive on (she once bought $60,000 worth of shoes in a single afternoon). On one memorable nine-day excursion to Iran, she and her entourage ran up *$600,000* worth of charges, all of which Onassis paid; nothing, perhaps, better sums up their marriage and their individual natures than their first Christmas together, when Ari gave her a $300,000 pair of diamond earrings—and Jackie gave him a pen-and-ink portrait of his yacht.

Even he, one of the wealthiest men in the world, was appalled at her spending—and her coldness—and they became estranged after less than a month of marriage. The purchases in no way declined. Indeed, Jackie sent spies to try to find out exactly how much he was worth, just as he set spies on her to keep track of her spending. She also tried to poison his own friends against him (without success). Inevitably Onassis returned to Maria Callas, who actually loved him and not merely his bankbook. He despised his wife in the end and began planning a divorce. By 1972 they were scarcely on speaking terms, and Onassis even contemplated the best revenge of all: speaking to reporters and informing all the world about Jackie's unholy avarice and excesses.

In January 1973, however, his son was killed in a plane crash and Onassis, the hard-bitten shipping tycoon, was devastated; he never fully recovered from the blow. And despite his involvement with Maria Callas, he was sometimes desperately lonely; one of the most powerful men in the world spent the Christmas of 1974 by himself, in his office, reading the newspapers.

Jackie and Christina Onassis arrive in Skorpios after Aristotle's death, 1975

Aristotle Onassis died in Paris of bronchial pneumonia on March 15, 1975. Jackie was not with him, but she arrived from New York, dry-eyed, several hours later. Despite the explicit nature of the prenuptial agreement, over which she had squabbled so lustily, and a will that Onassis had written shortly before his death, she still spent a year and a half in legal battles with Onassis's daughter, Christina, trying to receive more. Christina (who referred to Jackie as "the Merry Widow" and "the Black Widow") finally bought her off for $20 million—not because Jackie had a case but because Christina did not want to alienate Ted Kennedy. In all, according to C. David Heymann, Jackie "earned" some $42 million in her seven years with Onassis.[42] But now, at least, she and her children were set for life.

PRISONER OF FAME

IN THE WILD

Jackie Kennedy admired toughness and always feared that John would be too soft. (She told an employee close to the family that she was afraid he would "grow up to be a fruit."[43]) In October 1968 he enrolled at Collegiate, the oldest school in Manhattan but one (unlike more exclusive schools) with a mixed enrollment. He quickly became friendly with a schoolmate who taught him how to wrestle, and sports came increasingly to dominate his time. (In a repetition of one of his first acts at St. David's, John punched a fellow student in the nose shortly after his arrival until the offender stopped calling him John-John.)

His summers, however, though parts of them were usually spent on Skorpios, frequently consisted of a variety of training and "toughening"

courses for the next several years, even into his college days. In 1971, for example, it was Drake's Island Adventure Center off the Devon coast in Wales (sailing, canoeing, rock climbing, camping on the moors). He spent the summer of 1976 with his cousin Timothy Shriver (his other intimate friend in the family, along with Willie Smith) in Guatemala, which had been struck by an earthquake only four months before. The two boys wanted to do whatever they could to help—and they succeeded admirably:

John and Timothy slept on a rain-soaked tent floor, ate only tortillas and black beans, and washed in a stream. During the day John hauled sand, built outhouses, and dug trenches. At night he helped distribute food.

(above) John at the helm of a sailboat during an Outward Bound course in Maine, 1977

(opposite) John (third from right) and friends visit Palisades Amusement Park with Jackie, May 1969

Toughening up: During a visit to Aswan, Egypt, John and Aristotle ride camels, March 1974

"They ate what the people of Rabinal ate and dressed in Guatemalan clothes and slept in tents like most of the earthquake victims," said the Reverend Antonio Gomez y Gomez, a Catholic priest who directed the Family Integration Corps. "They did more for their country's image than a roomful of ambassadors." [44]

The next summer it was Outward Bound, a twenty-six-day survival course on an island off the coast of Maine. At one point he had to survive for three days with little water, no food, two matches, and a book on edible plants. (John vowed later that he would never go that hungry again.) In the summer of 1978 he spent six weeks as a wrangler at the Bar Cross Ranch in Wyoming. He never asked for any favors, did everything he was told, and impressed everyone not only with his prowess but also with his sense of humor. John was becoming more and more self-reliant, and his athletic skills were deepening.

He would need these skills, because the following summer came the most grueling test of all: the seventy-day National Outdoor Leadership Course on Mount Kenya, in Africa, where members were to learn how to survive deep in the heart of the jungle. At one point his group (half young women and half young men) got lost and the members appointed John their leader. He exhibited courage, maturity, and judgment even (or perhaps especially) in the face of a charging rhinoceros, and because he remained calm, the others did as well. Eventually the group was found by a Masai warrior sent out to retrieve them, but once again John's instructors were highly impressed.

So were the Special Forces divers with whom he spent the summer of 1983, diving off Cape Cod for the wreckage of an eighteenth-century pirate ship called the *Whydah.* This was the last of his great summer adventures, and by then all his physical skills had coalesced into a focused and disciplined whole. Whether John was a leader born or a leader made, he was now unquestionably a leader. If this was what his mother had had in mind, the training had paid off.

Background photo: The Collegiate School

John and friends leave the Beacon Theater in New York City, December 1974

IMPRISONMENT, OF SORTS

To be sure, not all of his life was this adventurous. Back in New York and at Collegiate, John was forced constantly to try to escape the prying eyes both of the public (at one point a nosy citizen, not realizing who he was, sidled up to John and started asking him what the Kennedy boy was like—John, with a straight face, said he was very nice indeed) and of the Secret Service, whose ministrations he was beginning to find oppressive. The agents were only doing their jobs, but their jobs entailed shadowing him everywhere he went; so eventually John and his classmates made a game of evading the eerie coverage.

John walks his two dogs in New York City with a Secret Service agent in tow, May 1972

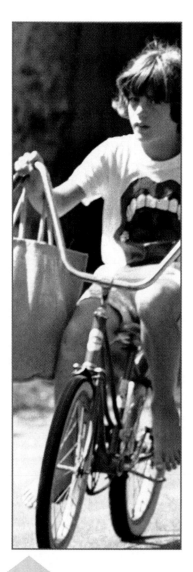

A bike ride to the beach, 1972

One jaunt landed him at the American Museum of Natural History; still another took him, at age fourteen, to see an R-rated film (but not a very racy one: Mel Brooks's *Blazing Saddles*). A third, however, made headlines around the world: John rode into Central Park, where the agents were wary of his wandering, on his expensive Italian bicycle—only to lose the bike to a mugger. Such incidents were a tremendous embarrassment to the Secret Service, which was required by law to follow him until he turned sixteen. John was as displeased as the Service, and felt himself to be in many ways a prisoner.

Imprisonment of another sort was looming, because the problem was not merely the general public that lined up outside his apartment house every morning and forced him to run a gauntlet in order to dash to a car and be driven to school. Even his instructors were awed and inadvertently made his life more difficult—especially when they asked him about politics and his "father's" programs. (He saw the same sort of thing years later in the Ivy League.) At the hands of such treatment, "John remained silent; this was his response to any outsider's mention of his father";[45] but it must have been acutely embarrassing to a child struggling desperately to lead a normal life.

There was no normal life for John Fitzgerald Kennedy Jr. Between death threats and paparazzi, bomb threats and rubber-neckers, Secret Service agents and star-struck teachers at his own private schools, he had little, if any, relief. In 1971 he (at eleven) was forced to give a deposition against Ron Galella, a scandal-sheet photographer even more obsessed with the family (especially Jackie) than most of his press colleagues. That same year he wanted to go to a summer camp with his friend Bob Cramer, but a bomb scare intervened, and the trip was canceled. And on top of everything else, there were always official and unofficial Kennedy functions to attend.

Then the rumors started to leak out about his father. A revisionist tendency set in in general, and the raptures that once had been sung about Camelot ("Washington seemed engaged in a collective effort to make itself brighter, gayer, more intellectual, more resolute. It was a golden interlude"[46]) now became carpings, readjustments, and wholesale assaults against the man, the mystique, and the policies. More difficult than that for his children, however, were the revelations about his womanizing.

Codes of honor were different in the 1960s. Newspapermen (they were always men back then) knew all about Kennedy's trysts and one-night stands and myriad affairs, many of them conducted in the White House occupied by his wife and two children, but in that galaxy far, far away a politician's private life was considered private and his amours were never splashed across the front (or even back) pages. In 1975, however, Judith Campbell Exner, failed actress, successful party girl, and former mistress of Frank Sinatra, Chicago mob boss Sam Giancana, and a host of others, began publicly discussing her affair with John Fitzgerald Kennedy, and that opened the floodgates. A slew of books and articles followed, including Exner's 1977 autobiography *My Story*, and suddenly Kennedy's relentless sexual past became fair game. He had been an obsessive and indefatigable skirt-chaser and now his teenage son and daughter had to deal with the knowledge that assailed them. The name Marilyn Monroe became particularly burdensome. (Jackie, who knew about at least some of her husband's affairs at the time and who certainly knew about Marilyn, had always gone livid at the mention of her name, and now, after all these years, the dead actress came back to haunt her yet again. John, during his school days, turned off the television whenever Marilyn appeared.) At first they refused to believe it and the Kennedy family (who had known perfectly well what was going on) vehemently denied the stories. Eventually, however, the weight of evidence overwhelmed all denials and the children had to face the truth. Jackie Onassis was profoundly upset. All this made life more trying for John.

KENNEDY TENSIONS

Still another source of friction, which again was caused by perception, much of it fueled by the media, came from his own family: not Jackie and Caroline, who were also victimized, but the Kennedys. John was very close to certain of his cousins, but many of the others bitterly resented him and his sister because they were presumed to be filthy rich. The jealousy only intensified when the press floated erroneous rumors that they had inherited a $15 million trust fund on Aristotle Onassis's death. John was subjected to

> Then the rumors started to leak out about his father.

John gets a "pitch" from baseball great Willie Mays of the New York Mets, June 1972

CHARACTER

JOHN KENNEDY ENTERED THE Phillips Exeter Academy in Andover, Massachusetts, the exclusive preparatory school catering to the intellectual and social elite, in the fall of 1976. Three years later he enrolled at Brown University in Providence, Rhode Island, a bastion of the Ivy League. In many respects his experiences at the two schools can be linked and the years blended together, because by now his character was coming into sharper and sharper focus, and it needed only a few finishing touches to complete the portrait. Andover supplied them and Brown perfected them; and it soon became clear that three primary interests governed his life: girls, acting, and sports, especially football. Perhaps, but not necessarily, in that order.

SCHOLARSHIP

John is not a scholar; many people have wondered if he is even very smart. Those who know him have never doubted his intelligence, and certainly he can handle himself adroitly in interviews. At other times, however, his answers seem unusually witless, but that may simply be because he is anxious to get the questioning over with and get those idiotic interviewers out of his face. Jamie Auchincloss, his stepuncle, pertinently noted early on that "John started life surrounded by the pageantry of the White House and hordes of people watching his every move, so it must have been particularly difficult for him to settle down and learn his ABCs."[48]

This seems to have been the crux of the

(above) John in New York City, May 1994

(opposite) A sigh of relief: John graduates from Phillips Exeter Academy, June 1979

"problem," if a problem there was. At Andover and Brown John was very restless; he rarely studied and frequently skipped classes and, despite his obvious intelligence, did not do well. He wanted to have a good time: He was more dedicated to parties and girls than to cracking the books. John even flunked math at Andover and was very embarrassed—though not embarrassed enough to mend his ways. He failed the bar exam twice before finally passing it on his third try (though he was also given preferential treatment and allowed to take the test in a private room); and he was always scattered and had difficulty concentrating. However, he is very bright and a quick study and did well as a prosecutor—when he applied himself. He doesn't apply himself often—but why should he? He is a Kennedy: He is constantly being called upon to go to functions, deliver speeches, open libraries, and support charities. He doesn't *have* to do anything; and since the only thing he ever really wanted to do was forbidden to him by his mother, as we shall see, why should he have bothered with the fuss and strain of study? Academics had never appealed to John. Athletics had.

SPORTS

He was always a sports buff and had a talent for many games, from kayaking to waterskiing, touch football to deep-sea diving, but even there his application was lacking. A family friend who taught him how to fish and sail said he had a great arm and could have been a quarterback. He was tough, rugged, highly coordinated, and superbly conditioned—though he never trained seriously enough to do anything with his talent. At Brown he joined the rugby team, but he showed up and played well only when he felt like it and goofed off the rest of the time. Had he dedicated himself he could have been a first-rate athlete. Instead, he merely developed a first-rate body.

EXHIBITIONISM

John Kennedy is notorious for having gone through Brown draped in a towel—and sometimes not even that much. He loved to skateboard around the Andover campus scantily clad and fre-

Background photo: Brown University

quently strolled around both schools bare-chested and in the shortest of shorts. He was very proud of his body and left little to the imagination. According to Couri Hay, who shared a gym with him on several occasions:

> I worked out with him and discovered John is a major exhibitionist. . . . He loves to walk around in the nude. He is in great shape and eager for everyone to see it. He walks around in the gym with his bathrobe open, and when he takes a shower he leaves the curtain open. . . .
>
> I remember there was a big party at Hyannis Port when John emerged

John gets some sun in Newport, September 1979

from the house dressed in only a towel—and then, completely naked, went swimming. Afterwards, he swaggered out of the water, real slow. Some of the waiters at the party were gay, so they couldn't take their eyes off him.[49]

Neither could the ladies: This has always been a major part of John's appeal. And women have been a major part of his life since he discovered them at the age of fifteen.

WOMEN

John is rich, handsome, stylish, athletic, everything—and his name is Kennedy. Furthermore, he is the best kind of Kennedy one can be: not merely *a* Kennedy, one of those irritating bunch who are difficult to tell apart and seem too frequently involved in scandals, but the son of the president slain in 1963. Women, even legal colleagues and trained lawyers, have always draped themselves over him, sometimes literally. They have tried to "help" him with his work. They have smiled encouragement at him nonstop. Often they have done far more. So has John. For the better part of twenty years he has been dedicated to studying the opposite sex—John's greatest academic triumph of all.

His women have ranged from intelligent, classic Ivy League types to Hollywood actresses (a family predilection), Brazilian pop stars, and the ultimate product of too many sexual fantasies, Madonna. By and large, however, he has favored clean-cut girls from good backgrounds, though not Daughters of the American Revolution. Christina Haag, for example, whom he met at Brown and dated off and on for several years, is a serious stage actress (whose career may actually have been hindered by her association with him): She was neither a Social Register debutante on the one hand nor a Hollywood bimbo on the other. Some of these girlfriends actually resembled his mother or his sister; most of them were the kind of women whom Jackie could endorse.

Jenny Christian, one of the first (and most serious) of his many girlfriends, became especially close to the family and above all to Jackie. She was glamorous, rich, and well-bred, the daughter of a successful Manhattan surgeon. She was also highly intelligent, much more studious than John, and an actress. They were a team for several years and John was very attracted to her, but their romance fizzled when she went away to Harvard to study psychology. Jenny seemingly was the epitome of the young woman Jackie wanted for John.

John is capable of chivalry, thoughtfulness, and even tenderness, and he generally remains on good terms with his ex-girlfriends (as opposed to his father, who once allegedly said to his brother-in-law Peter Lawford: "I want my women three different ways, and then I am done with them"[50]). Yet John can also be surprisingly thoughtless and wantonly randy; he seems constitutionally incapable of fidelity. He started dating Daryl Hannah while still involved with Christina Haag; one evening, when his affair with Hannah was in full swing, he put the make on Sinéad O'Connor. (Her response was to break his pen in two and stuff the pieces into his pocket.) Once he saw two different women on two different rendezvous at the Russian Tea Room—on the same night.

Despite all of his theoretical empathy, he seems to have little grasp of the mechanism of jealousy or of how deeply he can wound the women to whom he is supposedly attached. Christina Haag reportedly suffered from his behavior, yet she refuses to talk about him and is extremely respectful and even protective of his privacy. So are most of his lovers (and friends)—and those who do talk rarely have anything nasty to say.

His most publicized affair was with Daryl Hannah—fey, shy, and thoroughly confused (though whether this is genuine or a carefully calculated persona is unclear), with the air of a broken bird but the body of a blonde Amazon—who was living through a stormy liaison with rock singer Jackson Browne at the time. Hannah would pause, vacillate, move out on Browne, go back to Browne, pause, vacillate, move out on Browne once more; and John, so used to breaking hearts and treating his women equivocally, seems to have fallen hard for her. He catered to her every need, spoiled her (especially after Browne had allegedly beaten her), acted as white knight to her damsel in distress—a role he seems to enjoy. When Hannah finally announced that she was through with Browne for good, John wanted her to move in with him: He thought he had found his mate.

> John is capable of chivalry, thoughtfulness, and even tenderness, and he generally remains on good terms with his ex-girlfriends . . .

John and Darryl Hannah leave the wedding ceremony of his cousin Ted Kennedy Jr. on Block Island, Rhode Island, October 1993

Then Hannah went back to Browne and John was demoralized. When she suddenly left Browne again, John was ecstatic; and when Hannah was spotted picking up a used wedding dress at a Rose Bowl flea market in Southern California, rumors of an impending marriage to John stormed through the press. They only seemed confirmed when he invited her to the Clinton inauguration. She was also with him at the funeral of his mother.

Then it ended, or it fizzled out, or Hannah changed her mind again (some reports claim she was afraid of marrying a philandering Kennedy), or John couldn't finally commit—and once more he was left alone. This, however, was truly the end; some romantics contend that John left his heart with her. From his activity, though, it was difficult to tell because he was back in the saddle in no time, and has flitted from woman to woman since then. Undoubtedly the most bizarre item in his sexual history is Madonna, one of the most brilliant self-promoters in the history of show business.

(clockwise from top left):
Sarah Jessica Parker, Sinead
O'Connor, Madonna, and Xuxa

John attends a benefit premiere
of **The Fox and the Hound** *in*
Burbank, California, July 1981

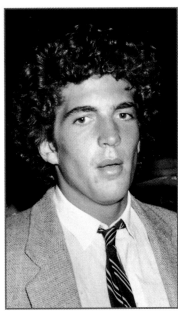

High on the list of Madonna's many obsessions is Marilyn Monroe, whom she wanted not merely to emulate but to *be*. Monroe, of course, had a very celebrated affair with Jack Kennedy (and a less celebrated one with Bobby), and Madonna, who wanted to inherit Marilyn's mantle in every way and absorb the actress into her own psyche (and body?), felt that having sex with John Fitzgerald Kennedy Jr. would be the ultimate fulfillment of her Monroe dream, the link that would complete the circle and make her truly one with the diva.

She chased after John without subtlety or relent, and he, though hesitant in the beginning, eventually submitted. Brassy types like Madonna are fairly the opposite of his ideal, but the two

AN ACTOR DESPAIRS

THE TROUBLE WITH JOHN, said Robert Kennedy's son David, was simply that he matured later than most. I also think the death of Aristotle Onassis hit him harder than people realize. . . . Then his mother pushed too hard, threatened him with a kind of emotional blackmail. If he behaved himself and did what she said, she held out the carrot. But she was also very quick in turning the cold shoulder. If he did something she didn't like, she would wave the whip. Basically, that's how she related to everyone. [51]

Already in his childhood John was something of a showoff and entertainer who enjoyed telling stories in a variety of accents, and he seems to have fallen in love with acting at an early age. Jackie was less than ecstatic from the very beginning.

(above) John at his cousin Michael Kennedy's wedding in New York City, March 1981

(opposite) John and his date take a ride at the Saint Anthony Festival in Little Italy, New York City

Even while he was in Manhattan at Collegiate she was uneasy. *The New York Times* took note of a school production of *Petticoats and Union Suits,* in which a fifteen-year-old John Kennedy appeared. His mother, wearing her trademark dark glasses, seemed nervous and annoyed. John was only fifteen. The next year he went off to Andover, and that is where his interest blossomed. John finally became serious about something that truly piqued his imagination, and he started spending less time with his buddies and more with the drama group.

According to his friend Wilson McCray, "John loved acting and if he hadn't been born a prince I think he'd love to have gone further with it." His drama coach, Holly Owen, had this to say: "If he had worked hard at it, he could have been a good professional actor."

him to that, given who and what he was. This is not the activity of a dilettante, which he has been in much of the rest of his life. Acting was different. Jackie, however, did not care. Indeed, she seems to have gone out of her way to humiliate her son. And although it is true that she was motivated to some extent by the fact that acting was a very *public* venue and would put her son even more squarely in the limelight (or in the crosshairs of a potential assassin's rifle), she also considered it beneath him. Acting was not respectable enough for a Kennedy. Being a lawyer was.

At Brown University John endured a very curious and embarrassing incident of which one cannot but suspect Jackie of being the villain. The production was *Volpone* and the critic of the *Brown Daily Herald* lauded John's performance. Subsequently, however, the critic publicly retracted his opinion (he actually said he regretted his praise) and explained that he had been sitting next to John's mother on opening night and must have been dazzled. John had made it clear to Jackie after the performance that he was serious about acting. Did the dazzling Jackie Kennedy Onassis then *suggest* that the critic change his mind?

John was bloodied but unbowed, and the following year he played Antonio in *The Tempest*. He received more and more flak from his mother, but his uncle, Peter Lawford, a mainstay of Hollywood second-leads for many years, encouraged him. He was the only one in the family to do so. "If a man wants to be an actor, he wants to be an actor," Lawford said. Jackie (who had always been a little in love with Peter and who may even have had a tiny fling with him in Hawaii in the mid-1960s) tartly scolded Lawford: She wanted her son to be, of all things, a scholar! (John seems to have been notably absent from *that* career decision.) Peter simply laughed.

In 1982 John's performance in David Rabe's *In the Boom Boom Room* was very well received, and the *Brown Daily Herald* did not retract its review this time. On the other hand, Mrs. Onassis was not present, although her daughter was. After that came John's most ambitious role to date, the lead in J.M. Synge's *The Playboy of the Western World*. Once again praise followed; once again Jackie was alarmed. He received superb reviews for his final Brown production, playing an Irish gangster in Miguel Piñero's *Short Eyes*.

By the time he graduated from Brown in 1983, John had made up his mind: He wanted to be a professional actor. Jackie was even more ferociously opposed. He was a Kennedy, the son of Jack Kennedy, the son of a murdered president, and as such he had an obligation to pursue a "worthwhile career." That which had been good enough for Humphrey Bogart (who had also attended Andover), Charles Laughton, Richard Burton, and a host of others was not good enough for him.

John, for once, persisted (this is another sign of his dedication, because not for the world, under any other circumstances, would he have hurt his mother—who had no qualms about hurting him) and said he wanted to apply to the Yale Drama School.

Jackie's response: "I'll disinherit you unless you go to law school."[55]

At that point John abandoned the attempt.

We can blame him if we feel like it, but how many of us have ever been in a position to be cut off from *millions of dollars*—Kennedy millions and Onassis millions—if we persisted in a certain course? And how many of us would continue in that course regardless, particularly when it would result in a breach with a beloved parent? We all like to think we would, but only very few

> He received superb reviews for his final Brown production, playing an Irish gangster in Miguel Piñero's *Short Eyes*.

John and Caroline at a benefit premiere of **Old Gringo**, *October 1989*

John attends **Pounding Nails in My Forehead**, *an Eric Bogosian comedy, in New York City*

Graduation day at Brown University, June 1983

could really do so. John Kennedy did not—and he has been without direction until very recently.

There are four footnotes to this history:

On Christmas Eve 1984, Peter Lawford died. John was now without a friend in the family who understood his artistic aspirations.

On August 14, 1985, John made his professional acting debut (and swan song) in Brian Friel's *Winners* at the Irish Arts Center in Manhattan. This was a final thespian fling before he went off to law school. Jackie was still terrified that he might do what he wanted to do with his life, so she "made certain that reviewers were not permitted"[56] and did everything in her power to steer everyone she knew away from the six performances. She and Caroline actually boycotted the play. On the other hand, a few of John's cousins—Willie Smith, Kara Kennedy, Bobby Kennedy Jr.,

John and Christina Haag after a performance of Winners *in New York City*

Tony Radziwill—attended and encouraged him heartily. His costars also urged him to continue with the stage, and there were numerous offers to move the play to Broadway. But Jackie's mind (and thus John's) was made up.

Several of John's former girlfriends have been serious actresses, including Jenny Christian and Christina Haag (who also appeared in *Winners*). Indeed, according to Barbara Gibson, "*all* the women who have been important to him earn their living from either the stage or the screen."[57] By keeping in touch with them, John has managed to keep in touch vicariously with the theater. (He is also a member of the board of Naked Angels, a high-society theater company.)

John made one cameo appearance as a "Guitar Playing Romeo" in a small independent film called *A Matter of Degrees*. Christina Haag also appeared. The film is available on video, though it is so obscure that you may find it difficult to obtain.

WANDERING
IN THE DESERT

THE LAW
The rest of the story can be quickly told. John took an extended vacation to India (where for the first time in his life he encountered no newspaper reporters) and was out of the country during the circus surrounding the twentieth anniversary of his father's assassination. Then he took a $20,000-a-year job as assistant to the New York Commissioner of Business Development, where he worked hard but betrayed little knowledge of day-to-day business or life.

Eventually, in 1986 he did as his mother wanted and enrolled in law school at New York University; clerked with the Civil Rights Division of the Justice Department in the summer of 1987, a plum assignment his grades did not merit; and interned the following summer in the Los Angeles law firm of Manatt, Phelps, Rothenberg, and Philips. Again nepotism was

charged: Those chosen for this prestigious firm were usually the cream of their law schools, which John was not. Charles Manatt, however, had been Ted Kennedy's roommate at Harvard. John's experience there was typical.

A party was thrown to introduce the new recruits, and female attorneys and interns rushed the conference room in droves before he even arrived. When he did so he was annoyed by the scene and ignored his admirers as best he could, fraternizing with the men of the firm. The men, however, were jealous and bitter: Who was John Kennedy to deserve all this ridiculous attention and sweep away all the good-looking girls?

He was doomed with one half of the firm before he even began; the other half could not have cared less what he did—so long as he did it with them. Female callers inundated the

(above) John in New York City, 1992

(opposite) John assisting his uncle Ted's campaign for the presidency, December 1979

John in New York City, late 1970s

switchboard; the men grumbled that he was given only easy (and fun) assignments and *still* didn't handle them well; and John's work, as always (except in his acting), remained mediocre. He didn't want to be a lawyer and had no particular talent for the law; but even if he had been inspired, how much work could he have accomplished with his female colleagues constantly chasing after him?

In any event he graduated from law school in 1989 and went to work in the New York district attorney's office ("I'm looking forward to seeing how good-looking he is," murmured one colleague) on low-level cases, which is standard procedure for legal novices. He and sixty-seven others were to be thoroughly trained over a three-year period, but they would not be allowed to prosecute until they passed the bar exam. John, as the world knows ("Hunk Flunks!"), failed twice.

Lack of study or lack of interest? Who knows? But the country took an avid interest in his doings:

> He was chastised by newsstand dealers and strangers passing him on the street. The most humorous story, which may be apocryphal, was of him walking in his West Side neighborhood. A homeless man was lying on the sidewalk, watching the passers-by. When he recognized Kennedy, he raised his head and said, "You should be home studying." According to the story, John admitted, "You're right."[58]

Eventually he passed the bar, prosecuted cases (but when he was prosecuting, the opposition made it personal: they cared less about their clients than about kicking John Kennedy's ass), won friends and admiration from colleagues, and left after four years. He had made no real mark. He never would have. John Kennedy was not built for the law.

POLITICS?

John F. Kennedy Jr., *as* John F. Kennedy Jr., has been forced to be interested in politics to some degree, but he has demonstrated only marginally more interest there than he has in the law until very recently, and obliquely.

He made his first major speech in October 1979 when the Kennedy Library was dedicated in Dorchester, Massachusetts. The following year he campaigned for his uncle Ted, but was surprisingly dull. In the summer of 1981 he worked at the Center for Democratic Policy in Washington, D.C. (research, fund-raising, and so forth), where women grabbed at him every time he appeared in public ("Now he understood for perhaps the first time that he was considered special, not for who he was or what he did, but because of a biological father he never really knew and certainly did not remember"[59]). At one point Ted urged him to hold a press conference to prove he was a serious person.

Jackie and Caroline attend John's graduation from New York University School of Law, May 1989

Background photo: New York University School of Law

President Clinton, Jackie, John, and Caroline at the JFK Library rededication, 1993

The main event was undoubtedly the 1988 Democratic National Convention where he introduced Ted and raised the roof. (It was on the heels of this speech that *People* magazine dubbed him "The Sexiest Man Alive.") Women were breathless and dewy-eyed and a rousing ovation ensued. And then?

Nothing. John spoke on the radio with Andrew Cuomo (son of New York governor Mario Cuomo), read from *Profiles in Courage* (proceeds to go to the Kennedy Library), established the Profile in Courage Award (for meritorious public service) with his sister, and helped set up a charity to aid students working with the handicapped. All this was noble and well intended, but none of it has had the impact that his simple name has had or his acting might have had. The 1988 convention speech, in Barbara Gibson's analysis,

was an obvious first step toward an implied passing of power. It was a way of bringing John more fully into the political arena. And it went nowhere. The moment was not particularly meaningful, and John has yet to prove himself either interested or comfortable in that arena.[60]

Will he ever? That is the $64,000 question. If so, "it is way, way down the road," according to John. "I haven't given politics much thought." Politics, however, never ceases thinking of him:

> John watched the [Clinton] inauguration enthralled. Observing the son of the thirty-fifth president stand with shining eyes, watching as the forty-second president of the United States was sworn in, some who had been close to John F. Kennedy remembered the presidency they had loved and lost. And watching John . . . some of the older Democrats who had seen the birth and death of Camelot looked at John F. Kennedy Jr., and wondered: Was he a bittersweet relic of the past or a vision of a future yet to unfold?
>
> He was the Prince of Camelot, and his birthright was undeniably political power. Yet he continued to sidestep his destiny, to delay the choice, to avoid the commitment.[61]

He did? Why was it his destiny? He was the son of a man who did not want to be a politician but who became president anyway

"I haven't given politics much thought."

Ted, Jackie, John, and Caroline at the Profile in Courage Awards at the JFK Library, 1992

The Kennedys chat with
President Clinton at the
rededication ceremony of
the JFK Library, 1993

and of a woman who loathed politics and preferred the arts (all of them except acting). How, then, is he *fated* to do the same? He wanted to be an actor, so why is he *avoiding* the commitment if he does not become the next Bill Clinton? Doesn't the world have enough politicians? And, given his record, what makes anyone think he would be any good—whatever being "good" in politics means today? As Barbara Gibson has noted:

He is the one Kennedy male who was never raised to be a politician. He is not comfortable with the theatrical atmosphere and adoration that comes from high-profile politics. He is desirable as a candidate because of his looks and his name, not because of his brilliance, his education, or his knowledge of solutions to social ills.[62]

Several of his much-maligned cousins are considerably more serious and driven in the field of remedying social ills than he is. Perhaps we should stop blaming John Kennedy for not claiming his principality and ask ourselves why it is so important to us that he do so. "Some are born great, some achieve greatness, and some have greatness thrust upon 'em," wrote a man far wiser than any politician alive today, but John Kennedy may have slipped through all of Shakespeare's cracks. He had his desire, if not necessarily his greatness, snatched away from him, admittedly with his own acquiescence in the end. Who are we to demand that he have another thrust where it is not welcome? Certainly we have no right to try to pigeonhole him, because he has managed to blindside us all, as recent events have shown.

A NEW BEGINNING?

ON MAY 19, 1994, JACKIE Kennedy Onassis died of cancer after a relatively short struggle. The nation was shocked; Jackie herself had assumed that she would have several more months, if not several more years, before she finally succumbed. Her particular strain of lymphoma, however, proved surprisingly tenacious and aggressive; and as she was buried near her husband, Americans mourned. The last real link with Camelot was gone.

For a few days the nation relived its affection for the pillbox hats and the brilliant French fashions, and the hopes and ideals that the young, dazzling Kennedys had inspired; and John Kennedy Jr. quietly assumed the mantle of leadership within his family. He spoke eloquently, at the funeral and afterward, of his mother's deeds, her aspirations, and the values for which she stood; then he continued with the plan he had been mulling over for some time and had been carefully preparing for months. John Kennedy would not run for office, would not direct the battle from behind the scenes, would not advise or consent or in other ways make his presence known. Instead, he would do the completely unexpected, the entirely unpredictable, the one thing, perhaps, that would have seemed unthinkable, ridiculous, and out of the question even a few months before: He, a man hounded half to death by reporters throughout his life, would publish a magazine. (He vows not to delve into people's private lives.)

And not just any magazine: a magazine devoted to politics. And not just any magazine devoted to politics: "a lifestyle magazine with politics at its core, illuminating the points

(above) John walks along the beach at Hyannis Port, Massachusetts, January 1995

(opposite) John at the JFK Library rededication, 1993

John and Caroline watch as Jackie's casket is loaded into a hearse outside St. Ignatius Loyola Catholic Church in New York City, May 1994

John kisses his mother's coffin at Arlington National Cemetery, May 1994

where politics converges with business, media, entertainment, fashion, art and science."[63] A magazine that will not dryly analyze political trends or moan about the current state of affairs, but a glitzy, glossy, lively ensemble that will try to meld the styles of *People* and *Vanity Fair* and *Rolling Stone* into a whole focused always, in the end, on politics in one way or another.

That is the key: "in one way or another." Anyone can write about Bill Clinton now; *George* (named after our first president) wants to inform the electorate (now) about the unknowns and little-knowns who will be the Bill Clintons of the next decade, the dark horses and "out of nowheres" who will somehow seize voters and seize the imagination and seize the reigns of power. It will also profile pollsters, strategists, speechwriters, point men, lobbyists— all the "little" people and behind-the-scenes figures who direct campaigns, buy and sell and shape ideas, and influence elections directly and indirectly but who are rarely mentioned, photographed, or even acknowledged in public.

And *George* wants to be fun: John Kennedy is not about to bore readers with soporific graphics or articles or jeremiads and put a political nation to sleep. The maiden issue featured supermodel Cindy Crawford on the cover in George Washington–era drag; Crawford again, along with fashion designer Isaac Mizrahi, discussing the (generally dismal) fashions of Washington; Madonna,

initiating a regular feature in which celebrities from various fields will muse about "If I Were President"; a slew of articles on the Art of Politics (Julia Roberts in Haiti for UNICEF; inside a "dial session, where politicians troll for sound bites"; a guide to Washington's biggest leakers; and almost a dozen more); and a corresponding set of features on the Politics of Art (book reviews, film reviews, and articles on rock and roll, all slanted toward social and political concerns). In addition, there were longer features on Heather Higgins, Candace Gingrich, and Teresa Heinz—exactly the sort of unknowns who may be household names next month or year; analyses of Congress and the Republican Party; an interview with George Wallace (conducted by Kennedy himself, who plans to do interviews on a regular basis); and still more. It is a decidedly mixed bag by intention: The magazine's cofounders (Kennedy as editor-in-chief and Michael J. Berman as executive publisher) hope to offer at least *something* to everyone in every issue.

John in New York City, 1993

John after seeing Speed the Plow *in New York City, 1988*

George is resolutely nonpartisan despite Kennedy's obvious personal ties to the Democratic party. It is interested in informing and entertaining, in covering the intersection of politics and popular culture, not in waving banners or promoting individual candidates. *George* celebrates the idea of politics in general, not particular policies as such. Kennedy's critics consider this odd; he considers it obvious. *The Nation, The New Republic,* and other journals can do what they do; he saw "the opportunity to change the definition of a political magazine,"[64] and he has run with it. Advertisers have run with it as well.

John Kennedy is unique: He has access to people and financial backers (many of whom signed on to *George* only because Kennedy was involved) that no one else in the country has. There is probably not a politician in America (or an advertiser, a journalist, or a celebrity) who will not return his phone calls—up to and including President Clinton. This does not guarantee that *George* will be a success in the long run (the majority of start-up magazines fail within their first year), but it did lead to a spectacular debut.

Best of all for John Kennedy, he seems to be having fun. There is no questioning his dedication to the new enterprise, and he stresses over and over that *George*, for the foreseeable future, is his future: He does not consider it a stepping-stone to anything else or an oblique entry into the political arena. But despite all of his hard work, he is enjoying himself immensely—and his life seems to be discovering its own keel at last, publicly and personally.

On September 21, 1996, in a small, private ceremony (fewer than fifteen people in attendance) on Cumberland Island off the southeastern coast of Georgia, John Kennedy married his long-time girlfriend, Carolyn Bessette. Carolyn, twenty-nine years old, comes from Greenwich, Connecticut, graduated from Boston University, and until recently worked as a publicity agent for Calvin Klein Ltd. in New York City. Her relatively low profile, in contrast with John's public one, is likely to add more stability and normalcy to their life together.

Has John Kennedy truly found his niche? Can Carolyn urge him to settle down once and for all? Will *George* be his *professional* future, drawing together the major interests of its publisher's life—politics and entertainment? Only the future can tell. The present, however, is very bright for John Kennedy—on a path he has chosen for himself. And no one has the right to demand anything else.

> Best of all for John Kennedy, he seems to be having fun.

NOTES

STILL STANDING

1. Interview with Larry King, *Larry King Live*, September 29, 1995.
2. Wendy Leigh, P*rince Charming: The John F. Kennedy Jr. Story.* New York: Dutton, 1993, pp. 196–97.
3. Leigh, *Prince Charming*, p. 32.

THE KENNEDY DYNASTY

4. Garry Wills, *The Kennedy Imprisonment.* Boston: Little, Brown, 1981, 1982, p. 20.
5. Barbara Gibson with Ted Schwarz, *The Kennedys: The Third Generation.* New York: Thunder's Mouth Press, 1993, p. 49.
6. Wills, *The Kennedy Imprisonment*, p. 66.
7. Joe Kennedy, quoted in Nigel Hamilton, *JFK: Reckless Youth.* New York: Random House, 1992, p. 215.
8. This savagely sordid and tragic tale is recounted in considerable detail by Gibson, *The Kennedys*, especially pp. 94–102.
9. Leigh, *Prince Charming*, p. 18.

THE KENNEDY TRAGEDY

10. See Peter Collier and David Horowitz, *The Kennedys: An American Drama.* New York: Summit Books, 1984, p. 137.
11. Thomas C. Reeves, *A Question of Character: A Life of John F. Kennedy.* New York: The Free Press, 1991, p. 71.
12. Gibson, *The Kennedys*, pp. 124–26.
13. Wills, *The Kennedy Imprisonment,* p. 290.

JACK AND JACKIE

14. "Coming of Age: At 34, JFK Jr. Is Finally Trying to Make His Mark," *Newsweek*, August 14, 1995, p. 54.
15. James Burns, quoted in Kitty Kelley, *Jackie Oh!* New York: Ballantine Books, 1978; paperback reprint, 1979, p. 23.
16. This tortured history is followed in numerous sources. One of the more detailed is Gibson, *The Kennedys*, pp. 149–53. One of the most sensitive is in Wills, *The Kennedy Imprisonment*, passim.
17. William Butler Yeats, "In Memory of Major Robert Gregory," *The Collected Poems of W.B. Yeats.* New York: The Macmillan Company, Definitive Edition, 1956, p. 132.
18. Yeats, "A Prayer for My Daughter," *Collected Poems,* p. 187.
19. Joe Kennedy II, Bobby's oldest son, was driving one night in 1973 when he flipped over a borrowed Jeep. Several people were seriously injured, including his younger brother David. David's girlfriend was paralyzed for life from the waist down.
20. Bobby's son David.
21. William Kennedy Smith, found not guilty in a decision that took seventy-seven minutes.

WHITE HOUSE DAYS

22. Leigh, *Prince Charming*, p. 36.
23. Maud Shaw, quoted in ibid., p. 67.
24. C. David Heymann, *A Woman Named Jackie.* New York: Signet, 1989; paperback reprint, 1990, p. 269.
25. Kelley, *Jackie Oh!*, p. 168.
26. Leigh, *Prince Charming*, p. 45.
27. Interview with Larry King, *Larry King Live*, September 29, 1995.

LIKE FATHER, LIKE SON

28. Kelley, *Jackie Oh!*, p. 8.
29. Leigh, *Prince Charming*, p. 203.
30. Wills, *The Kennedy Imprisonment*, p. 65. In fact, seven of the Kennedy children—all of them except Joe Jr., who died during the war, and Rosemary, who was lobotomized—married.
31. If this sounds exaggerated, see Wills, *The Kennedy Imprisonment*, passim.
32. Quoted in Leigh, *Prince Charming*, p. 209.

IN NEW YORK

33. Eric F. Goldman, *The Tragedy of Lyndon Johnson.* New York: Alfred A. Knopf, 1969, p. 19.
34. Kelley, *Jackie Oh!*, p. 44.
35. Jackie Kennedy, quoted in Kelley, *Jackie Oh!*, pp. 278–79.
36. Kelley, *Jackie Oh!*, p. 255.

THE ONASSIS YEARS

37. Aristotle Onassis, quoted in Heymann, *A Woman Called Jackie*, p. 497.
38. Leigh, *Prince Charming*, p. 124.
39. Ibid., p. 127.
40. Costa Gratsos, quoted in Heymann, *A Woman Called Jackie*, pp. 527–28.
41. Heymann, *A Woman Called Jackie*, p. 508. Heymann spells out all the sordid minutiae in exuberant detail; see his index under "Onassis, Aristotle, and Jackie, prenuptial contract negotiations."
42. Ibid., p. 586.

PRISONER OF FAME

43. Heymann, *A Woman Called Jackie*, p. 609.
44. Leigh, *Prince Charming*, p. 181.
45. Ibid., p. 177.
46. Arthur M. Schlesinger Jr., quoted in Wills, *The Kennedy Imprisonment*, p. 140.
47. Leigh, *Prince Charming*, p. 212.

CHARACTER

48. Leigh, *Prince Charming*, p. 98.
49. Couri Hay, quoted in ibid., p. 262.
50. Quoted in Gibson, *The Kennedys*, p. 290.

AN ACTOR DESPAIRS

51. David Kennedy, quoted in Heymann, *A Woman Called Jackie*, p. 611.
52. All these quotations are drawn from Leigh, *Prince Charming*, pp. 184–85.
53. David Kennedy, quoted in Heymann, *A Woman Called Jackie*, p. 611.
54. Chris Harty, quoted in Leigh, *Prince Charming*, p. 223.
55. Jackie Kennedy Onassis, quoted in ibid., p. 227.
56. Gibson, *The Kennedys*, p. 285.
57. Ibid., p. 284. Italics mine.

WANDERING IN THE DESERT

58. Gibson, *The Kennedys*, p. 289.
59. Ibid., p. 287.
60. Ibid., p. 289.
61. Leigh, *Prince Charming*, p. 291.
62. Gibson, *The Kennedys*, p. 294–95.

A NEW BEGINNING?

63. John Kennedy, "Editor's Letter," *George*, Inaugural Issue, October/November 1995, pp. 9–10.
64. Interview with Larry King, *Larry King Live*, September 29, 1995.

BIBLIOGRAPHY

MAJOR SOURCES

"Coming of Age: At 34, JFK Jr. Is Finally Trying to Make His Mark," *Newsweek*, August 14, 1995.

Duffy, Martha. "A Profile in Courage," *Time*, May 30, 1994.

Friedman, Stanley. *The Kennedy Family Scrapbook*. New York: Grosset & Dunlap, 1978.

George. Inaugural Issue, October/November 1995.

Gibson, Barbara, with Ted Schwarz. *The Kennedys: The Third Generation*. New York: Thunder's Mouth Press, 1993.

Gross, Michael, "Citizen Kennedy," *Esquire*, vol. 124, no. 3 (September 1995).

Heymann, C. David. *A Woman Named Jackie*. New York: Signet, 1989; paperback reprint, 1990.

Kelley, Kitty. *Jackie Oh!* New York: Ballantine Books, 1978; paperback reprint, 1979.

Kennedy, John. Interview with Larry King. *Larry King Live*, September 29, 1995.

Kunhardt, Philip B., Jr., ed. *Life in Camelot*. Boston: Little, Brown, 1988.

Leigh, Wendy. *Prince Charming: The John F. Kennedy Jr. Story*. New York: Dutton, 1993.

Mead, Rebecca, "Magazine Camelot," *New York*, vol. 28, no. 31 (August 7, 1995).

Wills, Garry. *The Kennedy Imprisonment*. Boston: Little, Brown, 1981, 1982.

SECONDARY SOURCES

Collier, Peter, and David Horowitz. *The Kennedys: An American Drama*. New York: Summit Books, 1984.

Damore, Leo. *Senatorial Privilege: The Chappaquiddick Cover-up*. Washington, D.C.: Regnery Gateway, 1988.

Goldman, Eric F. *The Tragedy of Lyndon Johnson*. New York: Alfred A. Knopf, 1969.

Hamilton, Nigel. *JFK: Reckless Youth*. New York: Random House, 1992.

Lawford, Patricia Seaton, with Ted Schwarz. *The Peter Lawford Story: Life with the Kennedys, Monroe and the Rat Pack*. New York: Carroll & Graf, 1988.

Leamer, Laurence. *The Kennedy Women: The Saga of an American Family*. New York: Villard Books, 1994.

Reeves, Thomas C. *A Question of Character: A Life of John F. Kennedy*. New York: The Free Press, 1991.

Sorensen, Theodore C. *Kennedy*. New York: Harper & Row, 1965.

_____. *The Kennedy Legacy*. New York: The Macmillan Company, 1969.